SKILLSTUFF
The basic skills activity encyclopedia for teachers

Volume III · Reasoning

by KIDS' STUFF Authors
Imogene Forte
Joy MacKenzie

Copyright © 1981 by Incentive Publications, Inc. All Rights Reserved. No part of this publication may be reproduced, stored in a retrieval system, or transmitted, in any form or by any means, electronic, mechanical, photocopying, recording, or otherwise, without prior written permission of Incentive Publications, Inc., with the exception listed below.

All pages printed in **large type** are student pages, which are intended for reproduction, as are the game boards and patterns. Permission is hereby granted to the purchaser to reproduce these pages in quantities suitable for meeting yearly student needs.

Library of Congress Catalog Card Number: 80-81737
ISBN Number: 0-913916-81-1

Printed in Nashville, Tennessee
United States of America

by

Williams Printing Company

WHAT'S IN SKILLSTUFF REASONING?

The Skillstuff Check List is sequentially grouped into five basic skills and processes areas.
- Comprehension—finding out, recognizing, remembering, gaining knowledge
- Application—making use of the known in new, concrete situations
- Analysis—taking apart the unknown; seeing relationships
- Synthesis—putting together the new and/or problem-solving through original thinking
- Evaluation—making judgments (according to self-made or given standards or criteria, and as a result of logical thinking)

Model Activities—one or more for each skill

Teacher Lesson Plans—specific skills and processes objectives, preparation, and student directions

Student Work Sheets—ready for reproduction and use

Competency Reviews—informal mini achievement tests for each of the five areas

And Lots More—answer keys, a glossary, and teacher yellow pages offering problem-solving approaches, springboards to divergent thinking, encoding and decoding systems, symbols and signs, etc.

HOW TO USE SKILLSTUFF REASONING

To Teach Basic Reasoning Skills and Processes:
Use the check list to find out where kids are and what they need to do (you'll find blank ones ready for reproduction on the back of each section title page).

Select and use activities to meet individual or group needs (the indexed check list following the Table of Contents will speed up this step).

Use the Competency Reviews to determine if and to what extent each skill or process has been mastered.

Begin planning for the next cycle and start over!

THAT'S WHAT SKILLSTUFF REASONING IS ALL ABOUT.

- just one quick and easy approach to diagnostic/prescriptive instruction in basic reasoning skills and processes

    ...and to add flair and excitement unique to your own teaching style, use all yellow page goodies to design more and better games, work sheets, and individual and group tests and projects.

ACKNOWLEDGMENTS

Special acknowledgment is gratefully accorded

> ... to Mary Hamilton, who illustrated the book, and to Gayle Seaburg Harvey, whose artistic flair contributed to the cover and the section title pages,

> ... and once again, to Elaine Raphael for preserving editorial excellence.

TABLE OF CONTENTS

Skills and Processes Check List 11

COMPREHENSION SKILLS AND PROCESSES
    Comprehension Skills and Processes Check List 18
    Treasure Talk 19
    Listen Here! 20
    Sports Minded Match-Up 21
    Cats' Night Out 22
    Lost Partners 24
    You In A Box 25
    People Watching 26
    Moving Day for Monsters 27
    Any Way You Look At It 28
    Private Eye 29
    Guess Who 30
    All About Buster 32
    Ready, Set, Go! 33
    Ad Agency 35
    Nut Crackers 36
    More Than You Ever Wanted To Know About Nuts 37
    Wish You Were Here 38
    Facts Worth Filing 40
    Shopper's Special 41
    Learning Activities For the "Shopper's Special" Center 43
    A Trip To Be Remembered 44
    Itinerary For A Trip To Be Remembered 45
    Beautiful Hawaii (a multi-skill center) 46
        Hawaiian Recall 47
        Factually Speaking 48
        Beauty Beyond Description 49
        Where In Hawaii 50
    Comprehension Skills and Processes Competency Review 51

APPLICATION SKILLS AND PROCESSES
    Application Skills and Processes Check List 54
    Prime Time Players 55
    Comic Conclusions 60
    Krazy Kaleidoscope 61
    Round 'N Wiggly 62
    Where Did The Time Go? 63
    Watch The Fingers 64
    Feelings Illustrated 65
    Gifted Giving 66
    Gifted Giver's Diagram 67
    A Man's A Man For All That 68

Let's Face It!	69
Rock Critters	70
Boy-Oh-Boy, Bubbles!	71
Picture This	72
Survival Scheme (a multi-skill center)	75
Lost!	76
Presenting A Plan	77
Selection Limited	78
Emotion Inventory	79
Role Relationships	80
A Personal Experience	81
Great Inventions	82
It's A Kid's Life	83
Shipwrecked!	84
A Sight For Crossed Eyes	85
Say It With Words!	87
A Tour Too Good To Miss	88
Let Me Tell You	90
The Reporters' Reporter	91
Application Skills and Processes Competency Review	93

ANALYSIS SKILLS AND PROCESSES

Analysis Skills and Processes Check List	96
A Packing Problem	97
Do You Remember!	99
Classification Clarification	100
Closed For Inventory	101
Mystery Mansion	103
Which Is Which?	105
A Family Problem	106
It's All Class!	107
Logical Links	109
Body Language	110
Exit-Out	111
Who's In The Hat?	112
Speaking Of Surveys	114
Two Sides Of Me	115
Who Has The Button?	116
A Big Bag Buy	117
Quotable Quotes	119
Tale Of Two Cities	120
Analysis Skills and Processes Competency Review	123

SYNTHESIS SKILLS AND PROCESSES

Synthesis Skills and Processes Check List	126
To The Rescue	127
To Build A Boat	128

Land Of The Giants	129
What Is It?	130
Sentence Sense	134
Eye Can See!	135
Speaking Personally	136
The Word Machine	138
Meet The Gip	139
It's Reversible!	140
Mix and Match	141
In Short	142
Jungle Journey (a multi-skill interest center)	143
Pebble Beach	143
Valley Of The Little People	144
Billboard By-Pass	145
Critter Crossing	146
Field Of Flowers	147
It's Your Game	148
Perfect Packing	152
Coded Communication	153
Party Producer	155
Speech Maker's Workshop	157
Clem The Clod And His Eloquent Owl	159
Menace Minimized	160
How Inventive Are You?	161
Make Up A Measure	166
Improvement, Inc.	167
Willy-Nilly Nomenclature	169
Maximize A Menagerie	170
Maria's Dilemma	173
End-Of-Story	175
Picture It	176
Zany Authors	177
Web City	178
Criminal At Large	180
Gala Gathering	181
What Will I Do When	184
Synthesis Skills and Processes Competency Review	185

EVALUATION SKILLS AND PROCESSES

Evaluation Skills and Processes Check List	188
Something Important Is Happening Here	189
Prediction Vision	191
Cherish Is The Word	192
How Would You Feel?	193
Name The Business	195
Personal Camouflage	196
Ernest The Estimator	197

Rate Your Reading	198
Critically Speaking	199
Principal Power	200
Explanation In Order	202
In Defense Of A Chair	205
A Citizen Speaks!	206
Say It Isn't So!	207
Take A Position	208
Newspaper Know-How	210
Nuke Or Not?	212
Evaluation Skills and Processes Competency Review	213

ANSWERS/GLOSSARY

Competency Review Anwers	216
Activity Answers	217
Glossary	221

Teacher Yellow Pages 225

SKILLSTUFF: REASONING CHECKLIST

Student's Name	Grade	Date	Teacher's Name

I. COMPREHENSION SKILLS AND PROCESSES — SKILLSTUFF Activities

- ___ Listening — 19, 20, 55, 56, 57, 58, 59, 106
- ___ Matching — 21, 24, 105, 145
- ___ Recalling — 22, 23, 47, 99, 147
- ___ Reading — 24, 44, 45, 46, 60, 97, 98, 99, 117, 118, 173, 174, 210, 211
- ___ Collecting — 19, 25, 40, 41, 42, 43
- ___ Observing — 22, 23, 26, 29, 36
- ___ Labeling — 27, 68, 84, 110
- ___ Identifying — 26, 27, 28, 30, 31
- ___ Questioning — 32, 41, 42, 43
- ___ Discovering — 26, 33, 34, 144
- ___ Describing — 35, 36, 48, 82, 120, 121, 122, 141, 152, 155, 156, 200, 201
- ___ Researching — 37, 38, 39, 40
- ___ Locating — 26, 27, 44, 46, 48, 50
- ___ Defining — 46, 48, 85, 86, 205
- ___ Responding — 20, 46, 49

II. APPLICATION SKILLS AND PROCESSES   SKILLSTUFF Activities

____	Dramatizing	55, 56, 57, 58, 59, 80, 202, 203, 204
____	Sequencing	34, 60, 61, 66, 67, 77
____	Listing	41, 42, 43, 45, 62, 115, 120, 121, 122, 180, 181, 182, 183
____	Recording	40, 63, 71, 72, 73, 167, 168
____	Demonstrating	64
____	Illustrating	65, 69, 112, 113, 136, 137, 139, 141, 155, 156, 167, 168, 176
____	Sketching	66, 152
____	Diagramming	66, 67, 82, 178, 179
____	Brainstorming	68, 130, 131, 132, 133, 140, 167, 168
____	Translating	44, 45, 60, 64, 69, 87, 115, 146, 159
____	Constructing	70, 84
____	Experimenting	70, 71, 72, 73
____	Associating	21, 28, 29, 44, 45, 55, 56, 57, 58, 59, 65, 69, 74, 97, 98, 110, 146, 147
____	Surviving	75
____	Outlining	77
____	Explaining	34, 64, 77, 78, 81, 90, 109
____	Assembling	25, 55, 56, 57, 58, 59, 82, 85, 86, 100, 143, 148, 149, 150, 151
____	Interviewing	83, 129
____	Simulating	70, 84, 136, 137
____	Arranging	61, 70, 85, 86, 88, 89
____	Interpreting	65, 80, 87, 106, 114, 115, 127, 139, 160
____	Scheduling	88, 89
____	Reporting	91, 92, 114, 198

III. ANALYSIS SKILLS AND PROCESSES — SKILLSTUFF Activities

- ___ Categorizing — 91, 92, 97, 98, 100, 107, 108, 111
- ___ Inventorying — 101, 102
- ___ Calculating — 38, 39, 103, 104, 105, 109, 197
- ___ Separating — 105
- ___ Solving — 47, 75, 77, 85, 86, 87, 91, 92, 103, 104, 106, 116, 119, 146
- ___ Dissecting — 87, 109
- ___ Relating — 26, 81, 85, 86, 87, 91, 92, 105, 107, 108, 110
- ___ Differentiating — 28, 111, 130, 131, 132, 133, 210, 211
- ___ Comparing/Contrasting — 28, 36, 41, 42, 43, 50, 75, 112, 113, 120, 121, 122, 208, 209, 212
- ___ Surveying — 114
- ___ Abstracting — 32, 60, 81, 87, 115
- ___ Advertising — 35, 117, 118
- ___ Decoding — 119
- ___ Generalizing — 120, 121, 122

IV. SYNTHESIS SKILLS AND PROCESSES	SKILLSTUFF Activities
___ Inferring	69, 127, 145, 173, 174
___ Extending	36, 49, 63, 80, 107, 108, 110, 128, 129, 130, 131, 132, 133, 157, 158, 169
___ Imagining	74, 84, 101, 102, 129, 130, 131, 132, 133, 135, 136, 137, 175, 200, 201
___ Hypothesizing	106, 130, 131, 132, 133, 175
___ Rearranging	107, 108, 134, 144
___ Magnifying	80, 90, 106, 135
___ Formulating	138, 170, 171, 172, 206
___ Visualizing	32, 34, 49, 74, 139, 176, 178, 179
___ Reversing	140, 175
___ Combining	49, 141
___ Summarizing	83, 142, 157, 158, 193, 194, 199
___ Creating	66, 67, 85, 86, 115, 119, 138, 139, 148, 149, 150, 151, 189, 190
___ Designing	41, 42, 43, 117, 118, 148, 149, 150, 151, 152, 180, 195
___ Encoding	119, 153, 154
___ Producing	136, 137, 153, 154, 155, 156
___ Modifying	134, 157, 158, 167, 168, 207
___ Refining	159
___ Minimizing	160
___ Inventing	82, 161, 162, 163, 164, 165, 166
___ Substituting	169
___ Maximizing	170, 171, 172
___ Composing	35, 177
___ Conceptualizing	34, 148, 149, 150, 151, 153, 154, 170, 171, 172, 178, 179
___ Proposing	180, 206
___ Organizing	25, 40, 44, 45, 90, 114, 148, 149, 150, 151, 181, 182, 183, 184

V. EVALUATION SKILLS AND PROCESSES — SKILLSTUFF Activities

- ____ Valuing — 41, 42, 43, 44, 45, 78, 83, 189, 190, 192
- ____ Predicting — 191
- ____ Discussing — 41, 42, 43, 192
- ____ Selecting — 38, 39, 44, 45, 76, 78, 97, 98, 111, 112, 113, 115, 127, 192, 195
- ____ Projecting — 35, 66, 67, 117, 118, 155, 156, 160, 193, 194, 200, 201
- ____ Conjecturing — 32, 79, 83, 161, 162, 163, 164, 165, 166, 196, 202, 203, 204
- ____ Estimating — 38, 39, 71, 72, 73, 197
- ____ Rating — 198
- ____ Criticizing — 41, 42, 43, 199
- ____ Deciding — 63, 76, 77, 88, 89, 97, 98, 99, 100, 105, 184, 200, 201
- ____ Defending — 196, 205, 208, 209, 212
- ____ Recommending — 157, 158, 206
- ____ Disputing — 207, 208, 209
- ____ Debating — 208, 209
- ____ Editorializing — 210, 211
- ____ Judging — 63, 71, 72, 73, 88, 89, 207, 212

SKILLSTUFF

COMPREHENSION

SKILLSTUFF: REASONING CHECKLIST

Student's Name	Grade	Date	Teacher's Name

I. COMPREHENSION SKILLS AND PROCESSES　　　　　　SKILLSTUFF Activities

- ____ Listening
- ____ Matching
- ____ Recalling
- ____ Reading
- ____ Collecting
- ____ Observing
- ____ Labeling
- ____ Identifying
- ____ Questioning
- ____ Discovering
- ____ Describing
- ____ Researching
- ____ Locating
- ____ Defining
- ____ Responding

TREASURE TALK

Ask each of your friends, parents, and teachers this question: "If you could keep only two words in the whole English language, which two would you choose?" Write their favorites on the treasure chest below.

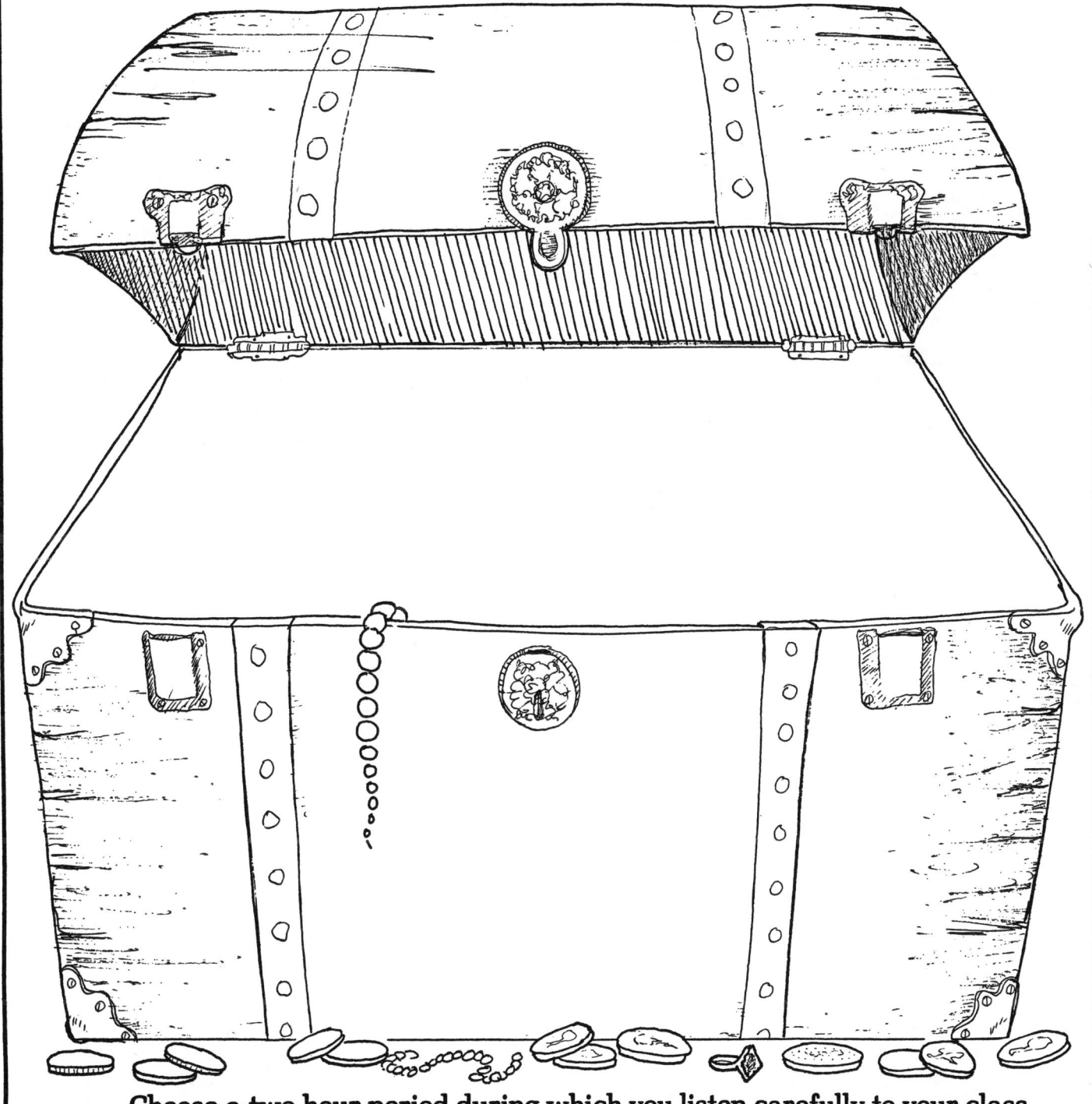

Choose a two-hour period during which you listen carefully to your classmates as they talk. Beside each word listed on your chest, write the number of times you heard it used.

LISTEN HERE!

PURPOSE: Listening

PREPARATION
1. Collect "sound making" items. Suggestions:

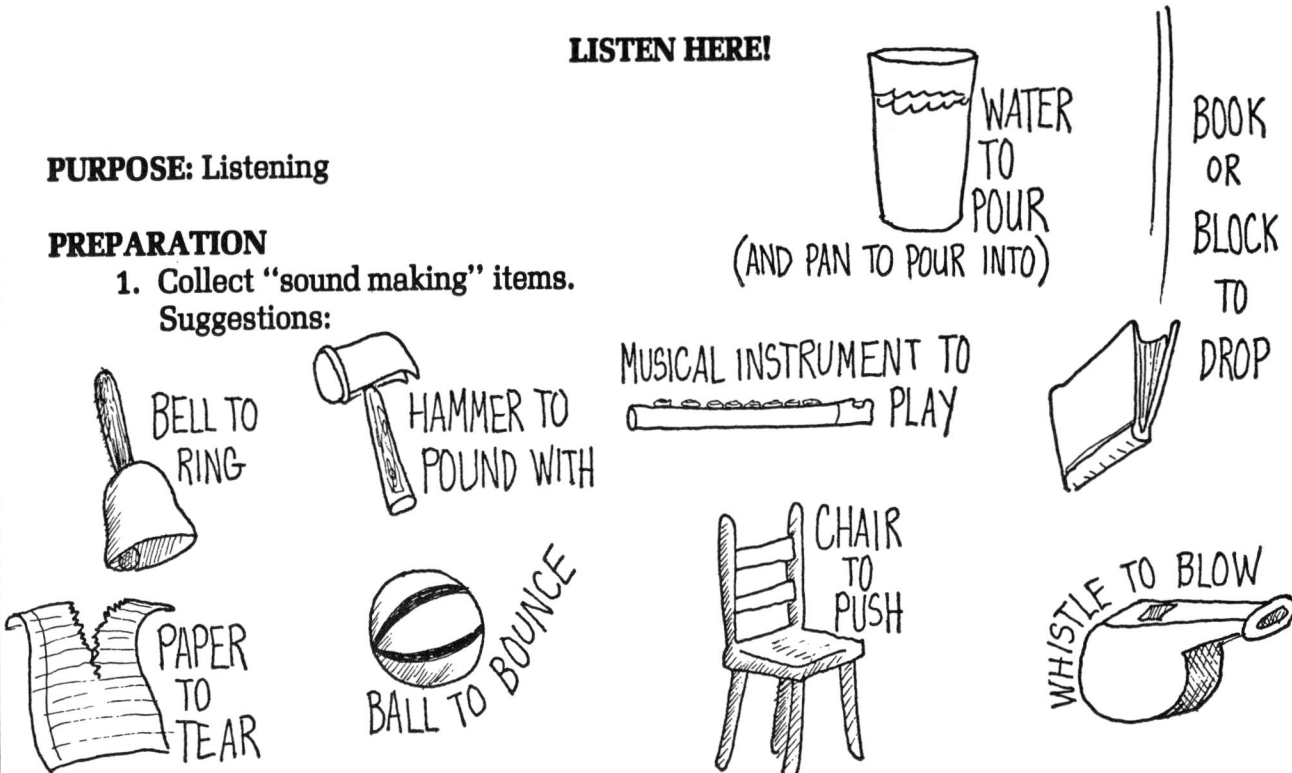

PROCEDURE
1. Blindfold one student at a time and ask him/her to identify the sound being made.

2. Select another student to be the "sound maker." Encourage sound makers to think of different kinds of sounds.

clapping	slamming drawer	laughing
tapping	scraping chalk on board	walking
sneezing	opening/closing door	running

3. When the blindfolded student correctly identifies the sound being made, he/she becomes the sound maker.

VARIATIONS
1. Direct the blindfolded student to identify 6 classmates by listening to each say, "Listen Here."

2. Present students with a tape of sounds (made by the teacher). Students listen to the tape and write answers on paper as the tape is played.

SPORTS MINDED MATCH-UP

Draw a line from each piece of sports equipment to the sport with which it is used.

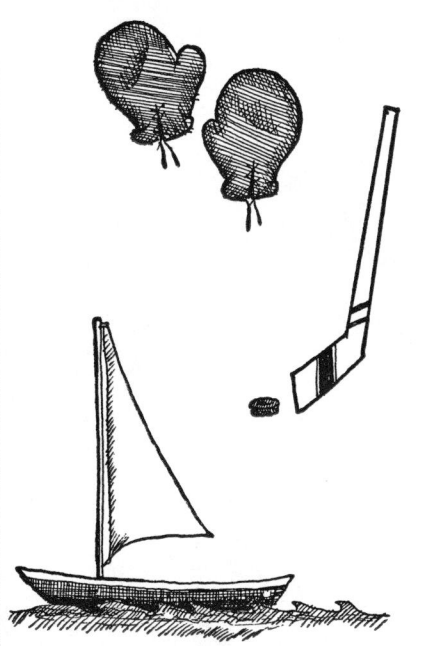
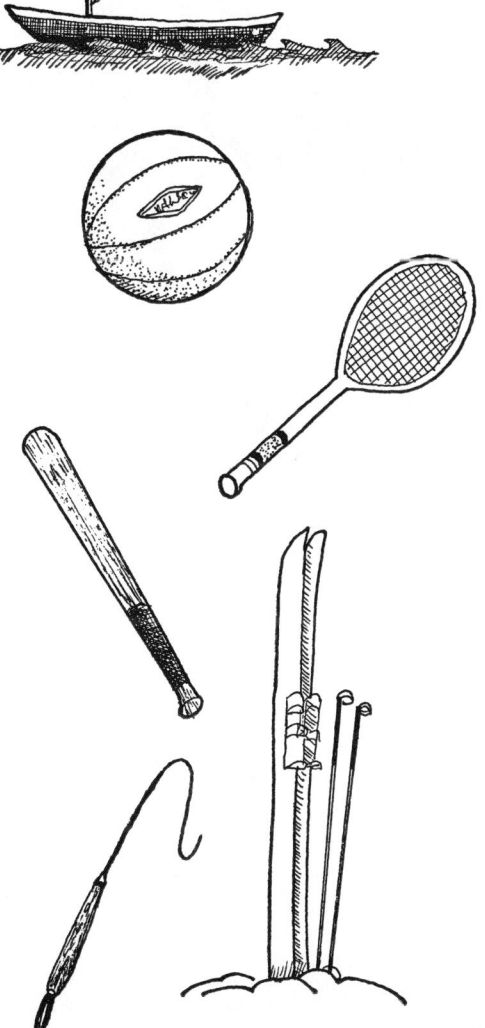
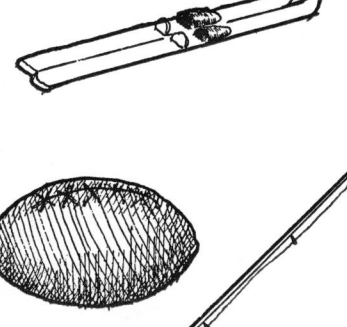
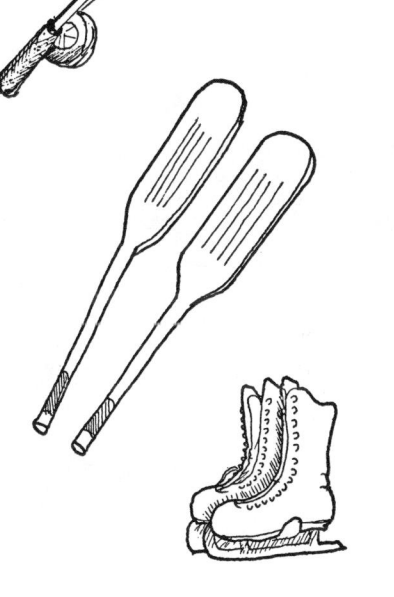

tennis

baseball

horseback riding

hockey

basketball

ice skating

sailing

golf

football

croquet

cross country skiing

fishing

canoeing

boxing

water skiing

21

CATS' NIGHT OUT

You have 5 minutes to study the picture below. Look carefully at each object in the picture. Then turn the picture face down and put it under your chair. Answer the questions on the next page.

22

Cats' Night Out, p. 2

Answer these questions without looking back at the picture.

1. How many mice are at the birthday party?
   _____

2. What are they using for a table?
   _____

3. What is the birthday mouse's name?
   _____

4. Is the cake chocolate or vanilla?
   _____

5. How many presents did you see?
   _____

6. Is the tablecloth polka dotted or checked?
   _____

7. Who are the uninvited guests?
   _____

8. Name two ways they are trying to sneak into the party.
   _____
   _____

9. Is the weather mostly cloudy or mostly sunny?
   _____

10. How many mice are wearing party hats?
    _____

11. How many cats are in the picture?
    _____

LOST PARTNERS

These partners made a terrible mistake and walked through a mirror. Now they have lost one another.

Hold this page up to a mirror and see if you can get them back together again. Join each pair of words with a line.

bat

Mom

hat

sister

sock

brother

Dad

shoe

ball

ham

coat

eggs

YOU IN A BOX

Take this list home with you. It will remind you of some things that you can collect that will help you tell a story about yourself without any words.

Try to find some of these.

- a picture of you
- a favorite small toy
- a sample of your handwriting
- a tiny piece of material from one of your shirts
- a leaf from the tree nearest your house
- your favorite small book
- a foot tracing of each person who lives in your house (use newspaper to trace the feet on)
- a list of 3 TV shows you have watched in the last week
- the box top from your favorite kind of cereal
- one of your special small treasures that you keep in your room

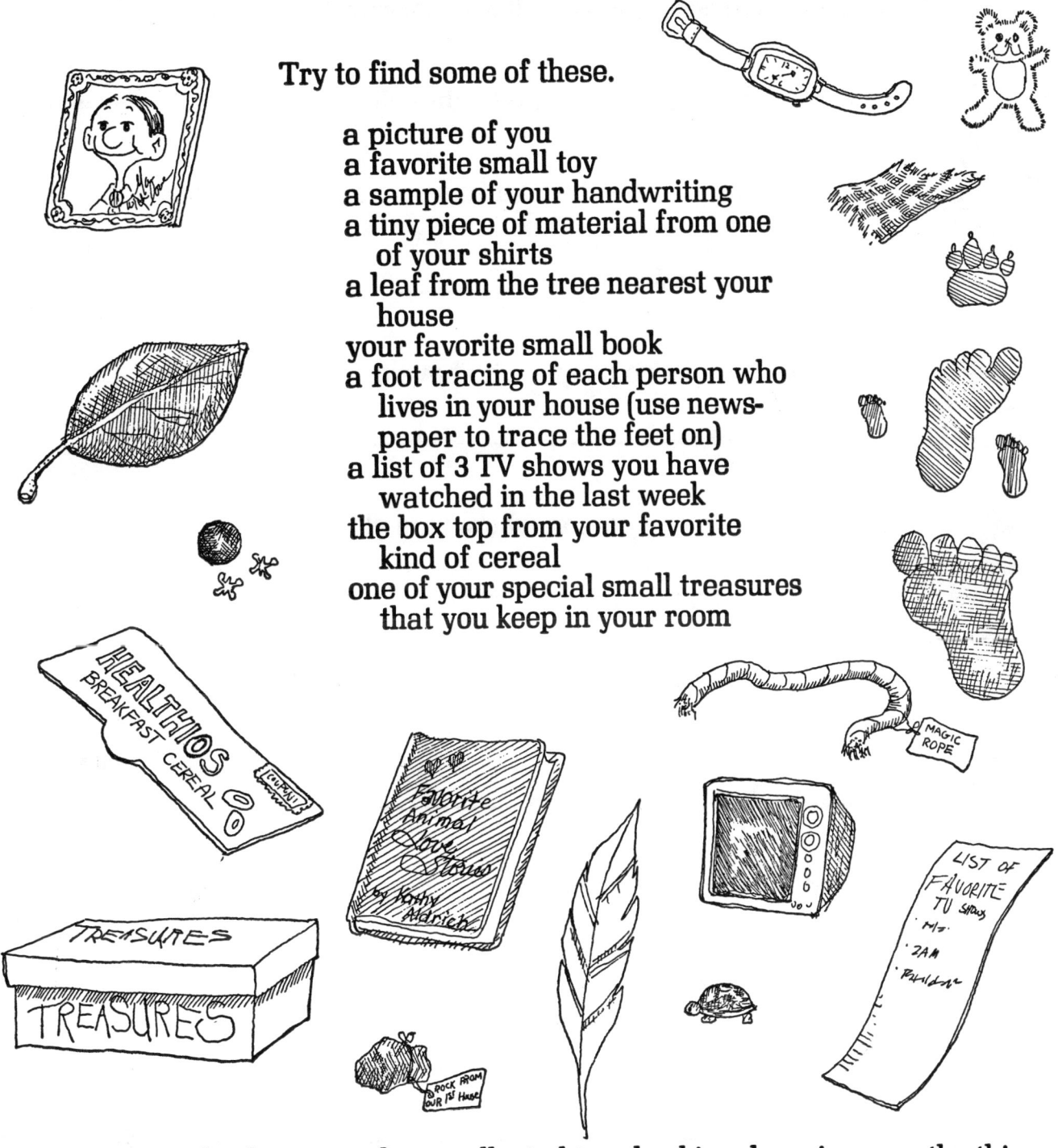

Bring the things you have collected to school in a box. Arrange the things you have brought neatly on your desk to make a display that tells about you.

Visit the displays of your classmates. Talk about what you have learned about each other.

People Watching

Looking carefully at something is called observing. Observe each person in your class. Then, complete these sentences.

1. A person who sits by me has on the color _____.

2. A boy who sits near the door has _____ hair.

3. The teacher looks very _____.

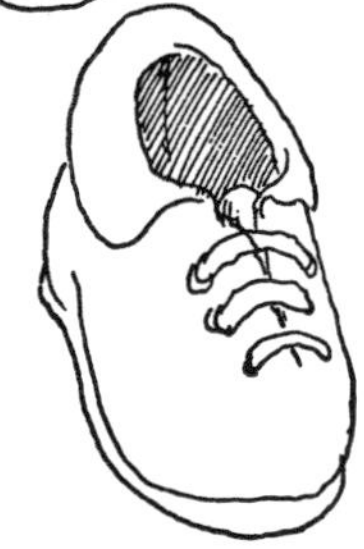

4. The names of two people who have on the same color shoes are _____ and _____.

5. The name of one person who wears glasses is _____.

6. _____ is wearing a shirt with buttons.

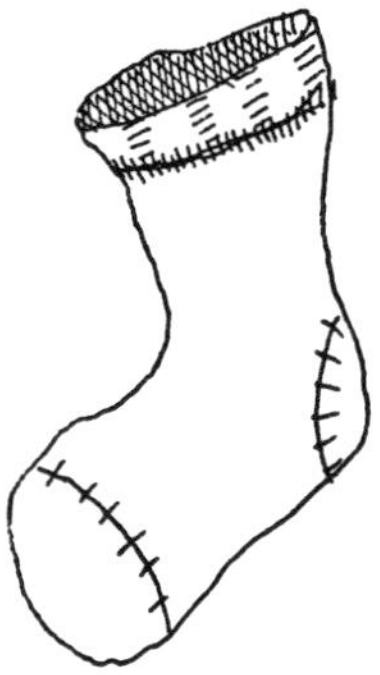

7. A girl who has blue eyes is _____.

8. In this room, there are _____ windows.

9. Someone I like very much has on _____ socks.

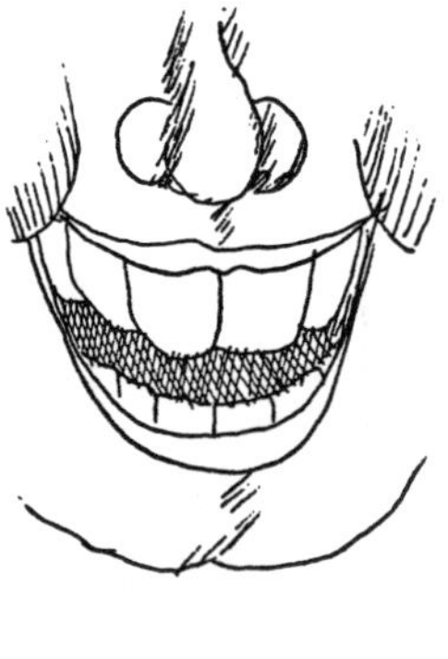

10. A boy sitting far away from me is wearing the color _____.

11. As I was observing, I saw two people smile. Their names are _____ and _____.

26

MOVING DAY FOR MONSTERS

It's moving time, and Mrs. Monster is very busy. Can you help her by labeling some boxes?

Look carefully at the contents of each box. Then, cut out the labels on the dotted lines, and paste each one in the correct place.

BONES	TEETH	POTS and PANS
TAILS	TOYS	MASKS
BOOTS	HAIR	

One label is missing.
Can you write the word for that one?

ANY WAY YOU LOOK AT IT

Look carefully at figures A, B, C, and D. They are repeated in various ways in the nine boxes below. Shade in with your pencil each figure as you identify it. (It may appear backward, forward, sideways, or upside down.)

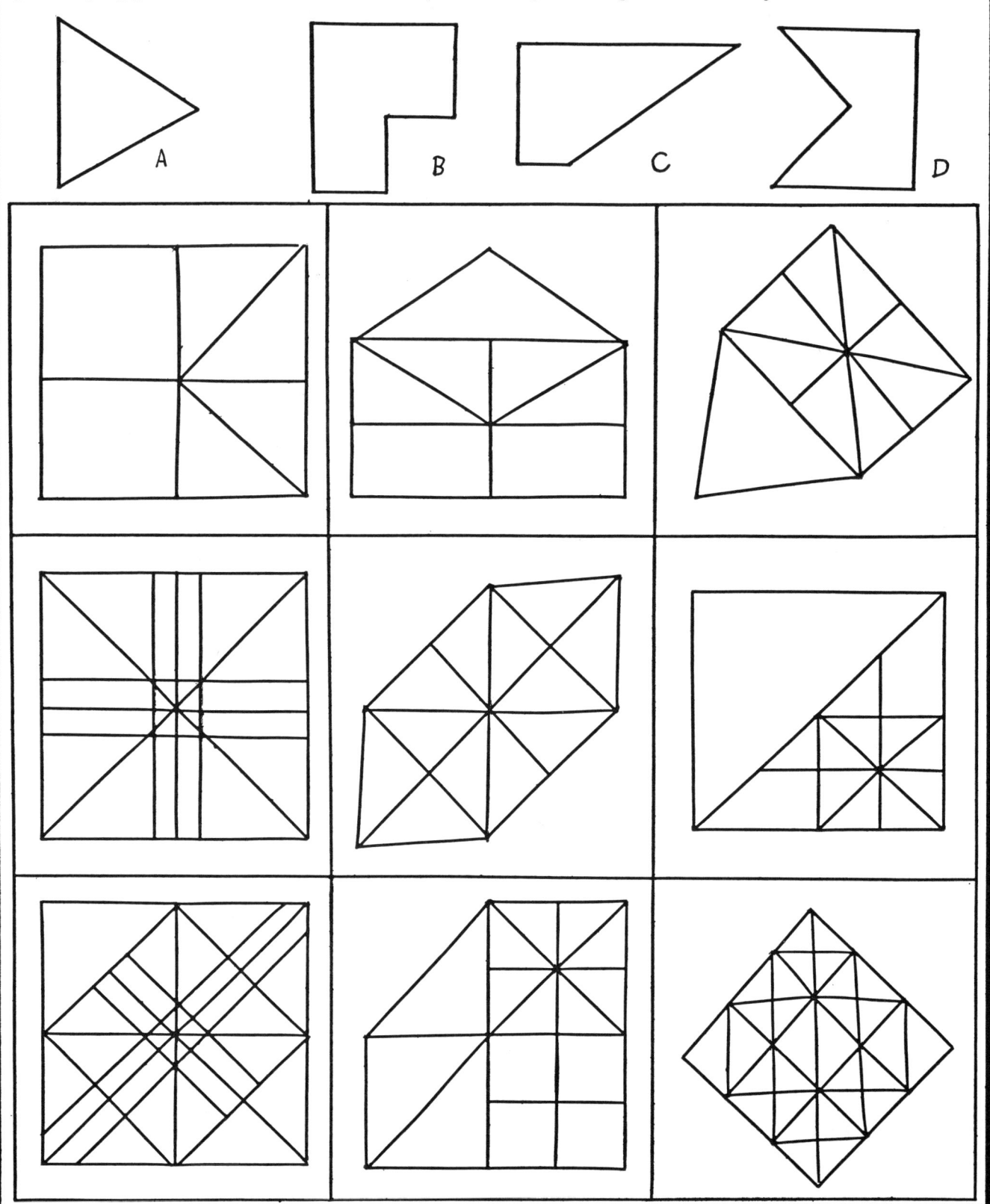

PRIVATE EYE

PURPOSE: Observing

PREPARATION
1. Ask each student to print his/her full name on a strip of paper. Place these strips in a basket or box.

2. Allow each student to draw a name from the basket. If a student draws his/her own name, that strip must be returned and the student must draw again.

3. Provide the following instructions.

PROCEDURE
1. Read the name you have drawn to make certain you know who it is you are going to observe.

2. Select any day of the week (Monday through Thursday) for your observation. Secretly observe and record your person's activities during the selected day. Carefully note times, places, and specific activities, like this:

9:22 a.m. – completed science learning center.
9:25 a.m. – stopped to talk to Johnny Jackson on the way to water fountain.
9:31 a.m. – returned to own desk.
9:32 – 9:40 a.m. – sat idly at desk staring out window.

3. Remember, a good private eye needs to be "under cover" and operate in secrecy. The success of your detective work will depend on the person being observed not knowing when he/she is being observed or who the observer is.

PURPOSE: Identifying

PREPARATION
1. Cut out letters to write "Guess Who" and large question marks from colorful construction paper to make an interesting and attractive bulletin board title.

2. Arrange the observation note sheets from the "Private Eye" activity on the bulletin board.

3. Pin strips of paper or tag board under each observation sheet so that students can write an identity "guess" for each one.

Guess Who, p. 2

PROCEDURE

1. Ask students to write a "guess who" under each observation sheet.

2. Hold free time discussions as to why each guess was made. Encourage students to try to remember traits and habits of various classmates in order to match correct identities with each observation sheet. This will really sharpen thinking skills.

3. It's fun for each student to learn new things about himself/herself from the carefully written, whole-day activity record, as well as to see himself/herself through others' eyes as classmates make true and false identifications.

ALL ABOUT BUSTER

This is Buster.
Buster is not like you at all.
Make up some questions to find out about Buster.
Write your questions on the lines below.

READY, SET, GO!

In just two minutes, David and Donnie will be late for school! Use your pencil to mark the shortest, most direct route for them to take.

Ready, Set, Go!

On this page, make up your own "Ready, Set, Go!" maze. Use a farm scene with 2 people, 4 animals, and other ideas of your own. Write your directions in the box at the bottom of the page.

DIRECTIONS:

AD AGENCY

People who work in advertising need to be alert, creative, and always on the lookout for new ideas. Look through some magazines for advertisements that capture your attention and make you want to run right out and buy the product advertised.

Select one of the products listed here to advertise. First, write a full description of the product, and then write ad copy containing "catchy" words and phrases to sell the product.

> heart-shaped bathtub
> mink-trimmed bikini
> rhinestone-studded lunch box
> strawberry-flavored shoe polish
> florescent ink pen that writes under water

— DESCRIPTION —

— AD COPY —

NUT CRACKERS

PURPOSE: Observing

PREPARATION

1. Collect four to six different kinds of whole nuts, and place them in a see-through container large enough so that each nut can lie flat on the bottom of the container without touching any other nut. Use peanuts, pecans, hickory nuts, hazel nuts, English walnuts, black walnuts, macadamia nuts, pistachio nuts, etc. (The number of nuts used should be determined by the students' ability and maturity levels.) To adapt this activity for handicapped students, use only one nut.

2. In a group discussion, ask the students to look carefully at the nuts in the container and describe each nut as fully as possible. At this point, the nuts are not to be removed from the container.

3. Discuss similarities and differences, names of nuts, colors, shapes, and other observations *only* as they are supplied by the students.

4. Tell students that the nuts will now be placed on a table for independent study.

5. Crack the nuts. Place the following study guide, some writing paper, and pens or pencils on the table with the nuts. Add two or three good reference books giving detailed information about the nuts.

Nut Crackers

MORE THAN YOU EVER WANTED TO KNOW ABOUT NUTS!

1. Take one nut at a time from the container and examine it carefully. Write down the name of the nut if you know it. If not, leave a space for the name to be filled in later. List the features that are immediately evident to you and the things that you know about the nut.

   Example: Pecan—1. oval in shape
   2. shiny shell
   3. light brown color
   4. mostly used for pies

2. After you have carefully studied all of the nuts, use the resource books to locate specific factual information about each nut. Find out:

   - where the nut grows
   - how its grown (on trees, bushes, underground)
   - if it grows wild or is cultivated
   - how it is harvested
   - how it is marketed
   - chief uses

Wish You Were Here

PURPOSE: Researching

PREPARATION
1. Provide stationery, post cards, and brochures from various hotels and resorts. It may take some time to collect all of this, but it makes a nice project for teacher and students. Maybe some friends outside the classroom will also contribute.

2. Add maps, globes, atlases, and reference books appropriate to students' ability and interest levels.

3. Provide the following directions.

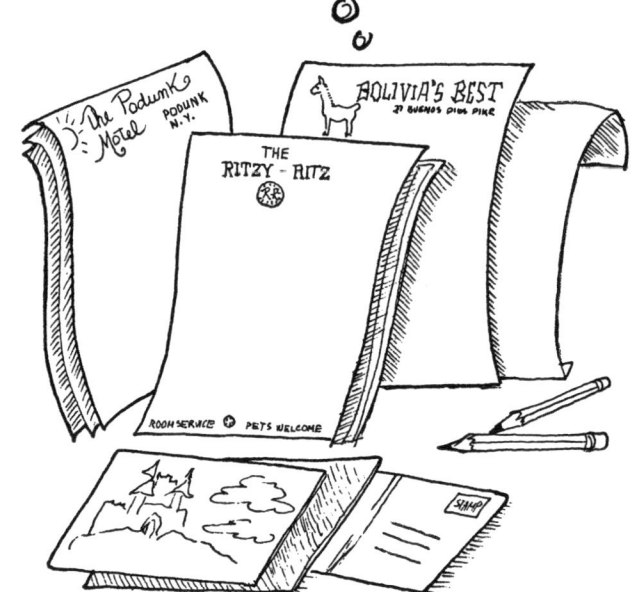

1. Select one hotel or resort to "visit."
2. Do the research necessary to help you tell all about the marvelous time you would surely be having if you were there before you write.
3. Use the stationery or post card from your chosen hotel or resort to write to a friend or relative.
4. Use the brochures, maps, atlases, and resource books to find information to complete the "Wish You Were Here" work sheet.

Wish You Were Here

Use the atlases, maps, and resource books to find *specific* answers to these questions. Do *not* guess.

Write the full name and address of the hotel or resort you have chosen in the space at the top of the work sheet.

_____

1. How many actual miles is it from your home to the hotel or resort?
   _____

2. Would it be best to travel to your destination by train, car, bus, or airplane? Why?
   _____
   _____

3. What will be the main type of recreation available to you?
   _____

4. What special sports or entertainment equipment do you need to take with you?
   _____
   _____

5. What kinds of clothes will you need to take?
   _____

6. Will your vacation costs be:

   cheap _____   average _____   expensive _____

7. Write a brief paragraph on the back of this sheet telling about the scenery you expect to see.

8. List the single most interesting thing you've found out about your vacation spot.
   _____

FACTS WORTH FILING

PURPOSE: Collecting important facts

PREPARATION
1. Select a topic of interest to the group, one that is out of the ordinary and not specifically related to topics generally studied at your level or locality. Ask students to contribute suggestions for a really exotic topic.

2. Secure a 5" x 7" card file box and packages of cards. Label the box "Facts Worth Filing About _____." Place the box in a spot which is convenient to the students.

PROCEDURE
1. Provide the following study guide.

    1. Try to find all the information you can about this topic. Use the library, reference books, magazines, newspapers, brochures, and any other sources you can think of.

    2. Record the information that you think is valuable and worth saving on cards for the file box. Be sure to give the exact source of your information, including page numbers. Sign your name at the bottom of the card and date it before you file it in the box.

2. At the end of a specified time, elect a committee to sort through the box and pick out the most interesting and informative cards. The committee will also organize the cards and present a report to the total group on why these facts were selected as worth remembering.

FOLLOW-UP ACTIVITIES
1. Come up with a creative way to organize and present the facts for a culminating project—a giant mural, a scrapbook, a party, etc.

2. Each student might select a topic of personal interest and collect "Facts Worth Filing" for an individual project.

SHOPPER'S SPECIAL

PURPOSE: Collecting

PREPARATION
1. Set aside classroom space for a "Shopper's Special" learning center.

PROCEDURE
1. Introduce the center with a class discussion focused on wise spending and the need for careful buying. List on the chalkboard ideas presented for saving money and receiving full value for money spent for consumer goods and services. Try to direct the discussion to immediate concerns of the students, taking into account spending patterns and life styles relevant to the group.

2. Ask students to help compose a list of objectives for the center. Make a chart stating these objectives.

Shopper's Special, p. 2

3. Ask one group of students to collect empty food containers to be used in the center.

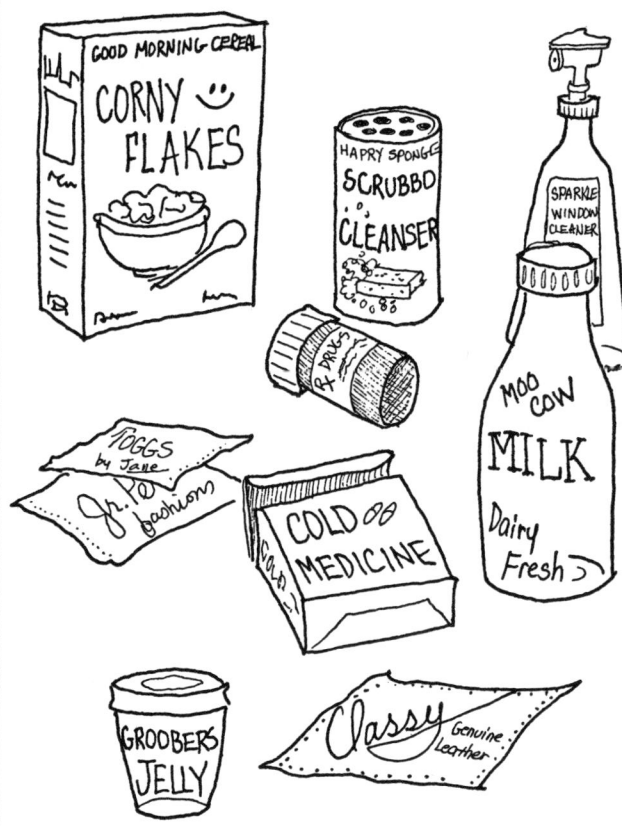

Ask another group of students to accept responsibility for collecting empty prescription medicine bottles, pill boxes, cardboard containers, and other health aid product packages.

A third group of students may be asked to bring labels from clothing, fabric, and leather products. In many instances, the labeled items will need to be brought because of the impracticality of removing the labels.

A fourth group may collect containers for household, automobile, and recreational cleaning supplies.

4. **Involve the students in developing criteria for selecting items for the collection:**

   . . . only empty, clean containers or items
   . . . no jagged or rough edges
   . . . all labels intact and legible
   . . . fits assigned category
   . . . permission of parent or guardian has been received for use of the container or item

Emphasize and discuss the importance of collecting items with the stated center objectives in mind, not just randomly picking up the first label or container available.

NOTE: For additional ideas and teaching suggestions, see *Cents-Abilities* by C. Farnette, I. Forte, and B. Harris, Incentive Publications, Inc., 1978.

LEARNING ACTIVITIES FOR THE "SHOPPER'S SPECIAL" CENTER

1. Compare labels of two different brands of food products (fruits, vegetables, cereal, coffee, tea, shortening, eggs). Determine which is the better buy and tell why.

2. Check labels to determine if all important information regarding use and care of the item is given.

3. Check labels for advertising "gimmicks." Question the accuracy and influence of such gimmicks.

4. Compare packages, and discuss the additional cost of an item due to packaging. Question the actual worth of the package, and think of some less expensive types of packaging.

5. List the different types of materials used in the packages, and discuss the sources and processes involved in production of the package.

6. Select one package from the center, and design a more attractive container for it.

7. Create a brand new product. Draw a picture to show it, list its ingredients, and make a label for it.

8. Develop an advertising slogan for selling a product in the center, or for a brand new, just invented product.

A TRIP TO BE REMEMBERED

Traveling is one of life's most rewarding experiences. Many people who can't actually pack up and go to faraway places becomes "armchair travelers." That is, they read and dream about the faraway places they'd like to visit.

Knowing where to get the right books, what to look for, and how to locate information are important to the "armchair traveler." It is just as important, however, to know how to organize the information for future use, and to take the time to do it. This helps the "armchair traveler" plan more effective trips.

There are many different areas of information you can study to learn about foreign countries. Match the branches of study shown here with the information you could expect to gain from them about any faraway place.

Now, select a country you would like to visit, and use information from the branches of study to help you plan a one-week trip to be remembered. Show your plan on the "Itinerary for a Trip to Be Remembered" page.

ITINERARY for A TRIP TO BE REMEMBERED

Always READ about the country you plan to visit before you go.

Things to THINK ABOUT:
1. Will you stay in hotels, inns, or in people's homes? Why?
2. What kind of money (names and denominations of coins and bills) is used in this country? Do you know how to convert your money into this country's currency? Don't forget to set up a budget!
3. Are there historical sites you want to visit?
4. What's the best way you can think of to get to know some of the people who live in this country?

	Travel From (city)	Travel To (city)	Means of Transportation	Things to See and Do
Day 1				
Day 2				
Day 3				
Day 4				
Day 5				
Day 6				
Day 7				

Beautiful Hawaii

Hawaii is the newest of the fifty United States, and is considered by many people to be the most beautiful state of all. It is 6,450 square miles in area, and is the 47th largest state. It is actually made up of a chain of islands, and is the only state in the union completely surrounded by water. The many beaches and miles of warm surf, the moderate temperature, the long hours of sunshine and beautiful sunsets, and the brilliantly colored flowers that bloom year round have made this state into a tourist spot sought out by people from all over the world.

The one hundred thirty-two islands range in size from the "Big Island" (also named Hawaii) to the tiny, uninhabited Kure Island. Trade winds blow from the northeast, and were responsible for the routes of sailing ships in days past. It is hard to believe that all these islands were built up by volcanic eruptions over a period of twenty-five million years.

Main products of Hawaii are pineapple, sugarcane, tropical fruits, coffee, macadamia nuts, and fish. Recreation and tourism are the main sources of income for many islanders.

The first settlers were Polynesians who sailed to Hawaii more than a thousand years ago. Since their voyage from distant shores in huge, twin-hulled canoes, their descendants have preserved many of their original traditions. These dances (including the hula), religions, chants, and customs contribute much to the beauty and richness of island life.

Over the years, new arrivals have come to seek their fortunes, build homes, and raise families, so the culture has taken on additional facets and flavors. For this reason, modern Hawaii is sometimes referred to as the "population melting pot of the world."

Beautiful Hawaii

HAWAIIAN RECALL

Solve the puzzle to find the hidden picture. Read each of the statements below. If a statement is true, color the numbered spaces as directed.

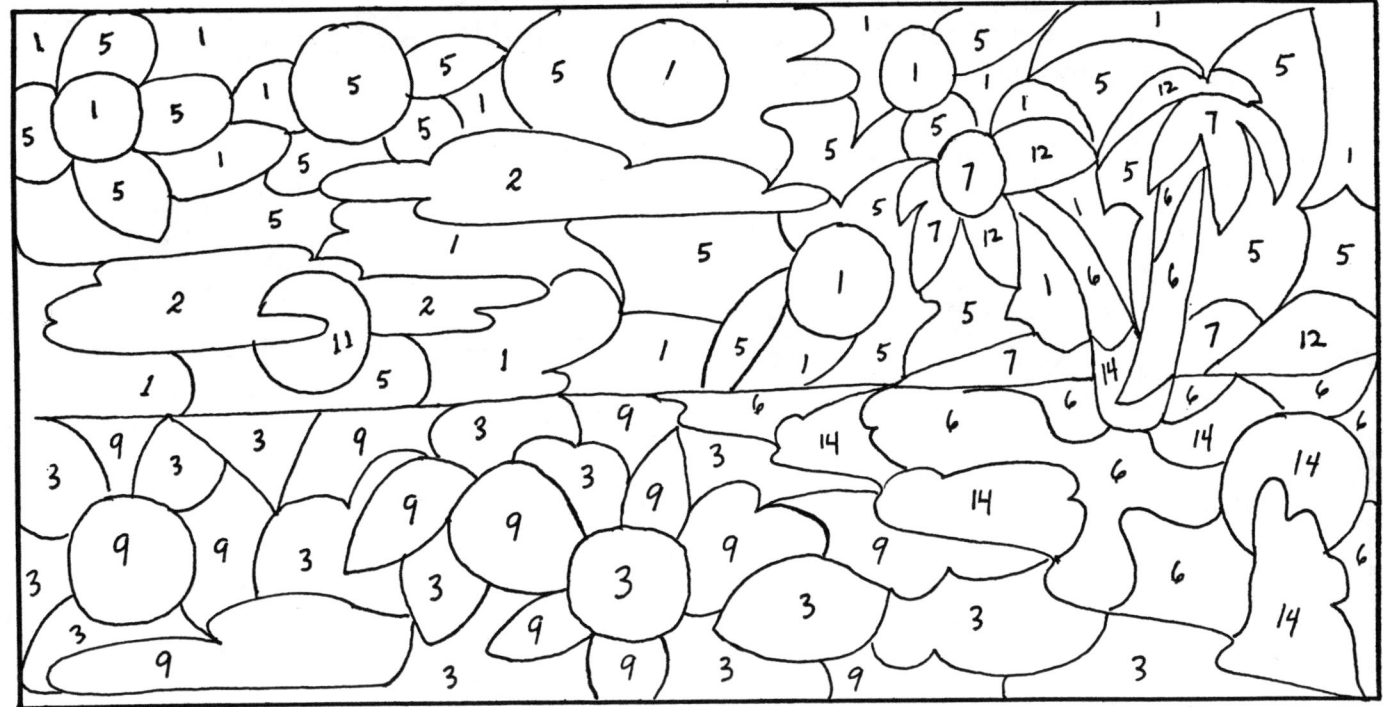

1. If Hawaii is a state, color the #1 spaces light blue.
2. If Hawaii was the 48th state admitted to the United States, color the #2 spaces purple.
3. If Hawaii is the only state in the United States completed surrounded by water, color the #3 spaces dark blue.
4. If the largest island in the Hawaiian chain is Kure, color the #4 spaces pink.
5. If Hawaii is made up of 132 islands, color the #5 spaces light blue.
6. If a chief source of income in Hawaii is tourism, color the #6 spaces brown.
7. If some citizens of Hawaii are descendants of the early Polynesians, color the #7 spaces green.
8. If potatoes are grown in Hawaii, color the #8 spaces red.
9. If Hawaii is really a chain of islands, color the #9 spaces dark blue.
10. If "Hawaii" means "little island," color the #10 spaces purple.
11. If the islands were built by volcanic eruptions, color the #11 spaces yellow.
12. If surgarcane is grown in Hawaii, color the #12 spaces green.
13. If the early Polynesians sailed to Hawaii in triple-hulled canoes, color the #13 spaces red.
14. If trade winds blow over Hawaii from the northeast, color the #14 spaces brown.
15. If Hawaii has a cold climate, color the #15 spaces orange.

Beautiful Hawaii

FACTUALLY SPEAKING

Reread the "Beautiful Hawaii" information sheet. As you read, underline the sentences that contain information you consider especially important in helping you understand the islands and islanders.

Use the information sheet, your dictionary, and the map to help you write good definitions for each of the following words or terms.

island — _____
_____

surf — _____
_____

volcanic eruptions — _____
_____
_____

trade winds — _____
_____

twin-hulled canoes — _____
_____

tourism — _____
_____

melting pot — _____
_____
_____

BEAUTY BEYOND DESCRIPTION

Beautiful Hawaii

Write a one-paragraph description of Hawaii that could be included in a geography text book. Use the information sheet and the map, but remember to use only facts.

___

DRAW PICTURES TO SHOW THREE PRODUCTS OR LAND FORMS THAT COULD BE USED AS ILLUSTRATIONS FOR THE GEOGRAPHY TEXT BOOK.

Beautiful Hawaii

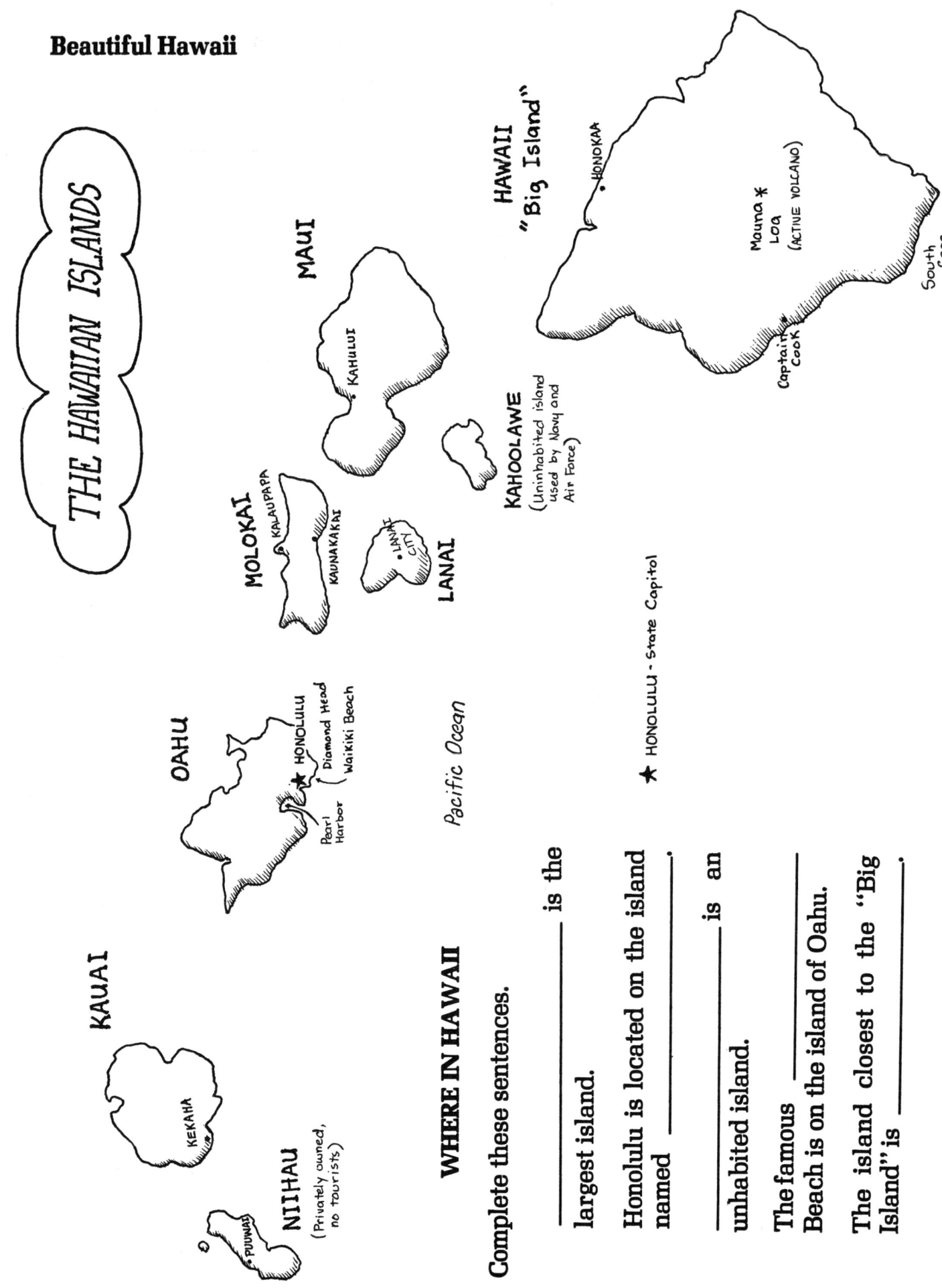

WHERE IN HAWAII

Complete these sentences.

_____ is the largest island.

Honolulu is located on the island named _____.

_____ is an unhabited island.

The famous _____ Beach is on the island of Oahu.

The island closest to the "Big Island" is _____.

COMPREHENSION COMPETENCY REVIEW

1. A certain silly squirrel sang ten top tunes at the circus.

   Read this sentence aloud to yourself. Circle the letters below that represent the two sounds you hear most often in the sentence.

   L   S   I   T   N

2. Circle the name of the sport below for which equipment is not pictured.

   skating
   boxing
   football

3. Circle the name of the month in which Thanksgiving is celebrated.

   September
   July
   November

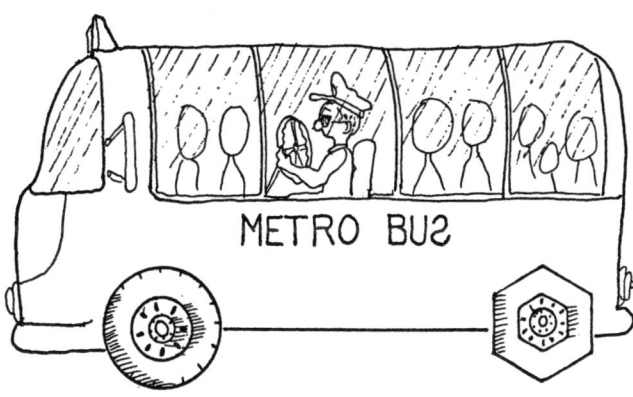

Look at the picture above, and read the following paragraph.

The bus driver stopped at the corner nearest the store. Three people got off, and one small girl and her mother got on. At the Fifth and Broadway stop, a photographer ran from his studio doorway at the last moment to leap on the bus, and almost knocked over a policeman who was helping an elderly man down the steps of the bus.

4. Circle the number of people mentioned in the above paragraph.

   7   9   6   4

5. If you took all of the words that begin with a vowel out of the above paragraph, how many empty spaces would you leave? Circle your answer.

   12   15   18   20

6. How many things do you observe that are incorrect on the picture of the bus? Circle your answer.

   2   3   4   6

7. Which person in the paragraph would you label as a "hurrier"? Circle your answer.

   the policeman
   the photographer
   the bus driver

8. Identify the person in the story who would be most likely to fit this description by circling your answer: gray hair, slight limp, glasses.

> elderly man
> policeman
> little girl

9. Put an X beside the one question below which is most likely to be answered correctly by a bus passenger.

___ How many of the bus passengers are over 21 years old?
___ Does the bus driver enjoy his job?
___ At which stop did you get on this bus?

10. Put an X beside the best way to discover whether or not this is an exceptionally busy day on the bus.

___ Ask the bus driver.
___ Ask three different passengers.
___ Ride the bus the rest of the day yourself.

11. If you wanted to prepare a report for your classmates about the schedules and services of this bus company, which of the following would not be helpful to you in your research? Put an X beside your answer.

___ Interviewing passengers
___ Reading maps of bus routes
___ Riding the bus one day a week
___ Reading about buses in the encyclopedia

12. Make an X beside the one item below that would not be good additional information to collect for your research report.

___ a sample bus ticket
___ a bus driver's hat
___ a timetable
___ a route map

13. Circle the letter that shows the point on the map at which you would get off the bus if you were going to the photographer's studio.

A   B   C   D

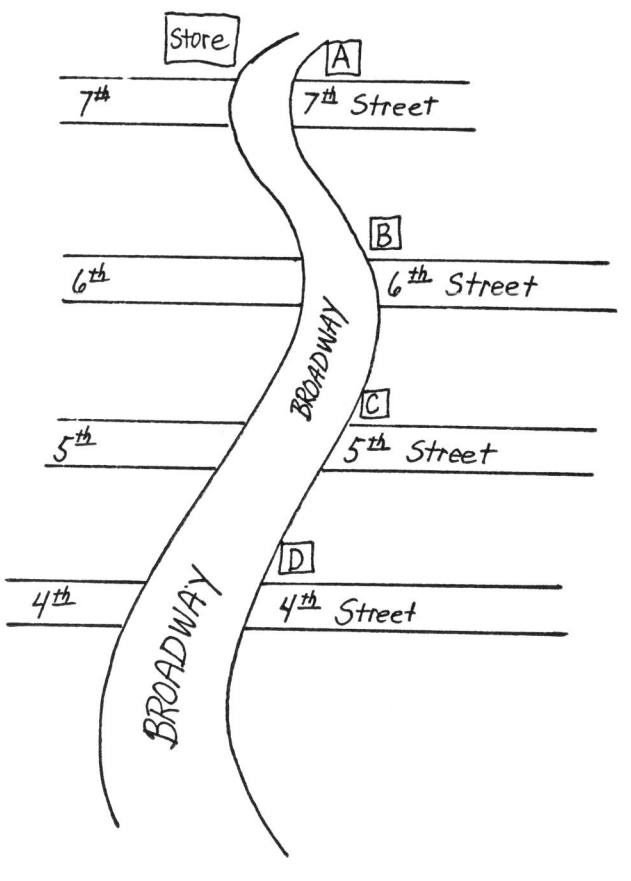

52

SKILLSTUFF

APPLICATION

II. APPLICATION SKILLS AND PROCESSES — SKILLSTUFF Activities

- ___ Dramatizing
- ___ Sequencing
- ___ Listing
- ___ Recording
- ___ Demonstrating
- ___ Illustrating
- ___ Sketching
- ___ Diagramming
- ___ Brainstorming
- ___ Translating
- ___ Constructing
- ___ Experimenting
- ___ Associating
- ___ Surviving
- ___ Outlining
- ___ Explaining
- ___ Assembling
- ___ Interviewing
- ___ Simulating
- ___ Arranging
- ___ Interpreting
- ___ Scheduling
- ___ Reporting

PRIME TIME PLAYERS

PURPOSE: Dramatizing

PREPARATION

1. Practice reading the story, "The Bremen Town Musicians," with exaggerated expression.

2. Color the props provided for each character and cut them out. (See the following pages.)

PROCEDURE

1. Choose 8 students to play the following parts: a donkey, a dog, a cat, a rooster, three robbers, and a robber-spy.

2. Give each character the props provided for his/her part.

3. Read the story aloud as a narration for a pantomime. Direct players to listen for their cues and dramatize the story as it proceeds.

4. After the dramatization has been done several times this way and the characters are familiar with their parts, allow them to say some of their own lines if they wish. (Older students may wish to take turns narrating the story.)

"The Bremen Town Musicians"

(Adapted from the story by Jakob and Wilhelm Grimm)

Once there was an old donkey whose master was about to turn him out or sell him for glue. Fearful of what might happen to him, he ran away and headed down the road toward a town called Bremen. "There," he thought, "I could surely be the town musician, for I can still bray very well."

He had gone some distance when he came upon an old cat that looked very sad. "My mistress tried to drown me," said the cat, "for she thinks I am too old to do her any good."

"Come along with me to Bremen," said the donkey. "We can make music together." So the two went along until they met an old hound dog whose master had threatened to kill him, and they persuaded him to join their singing group, too.

Later that day, the three came upon a cock sitting on a barnyard gate. The cock looked frightened. "The farmer's wife is going to cook me for Sunday dinner!" he crowed. "I must run away!"

"Come with us," chorused the three. So off they all went together to seek a new life and good fortune as the Bremen town musicians.

In the evening, they came upon a house where a light shone in the window. The four companions were very tired, and needed a comfortable place to rest. As the donkey was the largest, he went to the window and looked in. "What do you see?" asked the cock.

"I see a table covered with good things to eat and drink, and robbers sitting at it, laughing and talking."

"This is the place for us," agreed the four friends, and they began to plan how they would scare the robbers away.

They decided that the donkey would stand with his front feet on the window ledge. The hound would then jump on the donkey's back; the cat would climb up on the dog, and the cock would perch on top of the cat's head. Then they would all perform their music together.

So they took their places. Then, the donkey brayed, the hound barked, the cat meowed, and the cock crowed. With that, they burst through the window into the room and scared the robbers so badly that they ran out of the house into the forest.

The four friends sat down at the table and ate as if they would never have a chance to eat again. Then, full and happy, they each found a comfortable place to sleep.

The robbers, who were hiding in the woods, saw the lights go off in the house, and disgusted with themselves for being so easily frightened away, decided to send a spy back to inspect the house.

The spy crept quietly into the house and went to the kitchen to light a candle. He thought the shining, firey eyes of the cat on the hearth were live coals, and held a match to them. But the cat flew at his face, spitting and scratching. The robber spy ran for the door but the dog, who was sleeping there, bit his leg! As he ran out across the yard, the donkey gave him a kick in the pants. The rooster, watching from the rooftop, crowed loudly.

The robber spy ran back as fast as he could and reported to the leader, "A horrible witch sits in the kitchen and she spat at me and scratched me. By the door was a man with a knife who cut my leg, and out in the yard lies a big monster who beat me with a club. On the roof sits a judge who called out, 'Bring the thief to me!' So I ran away as fast as I could!"

The robbers decided to leave forever, but the four musicians stayed and lived in their house happily ever after.

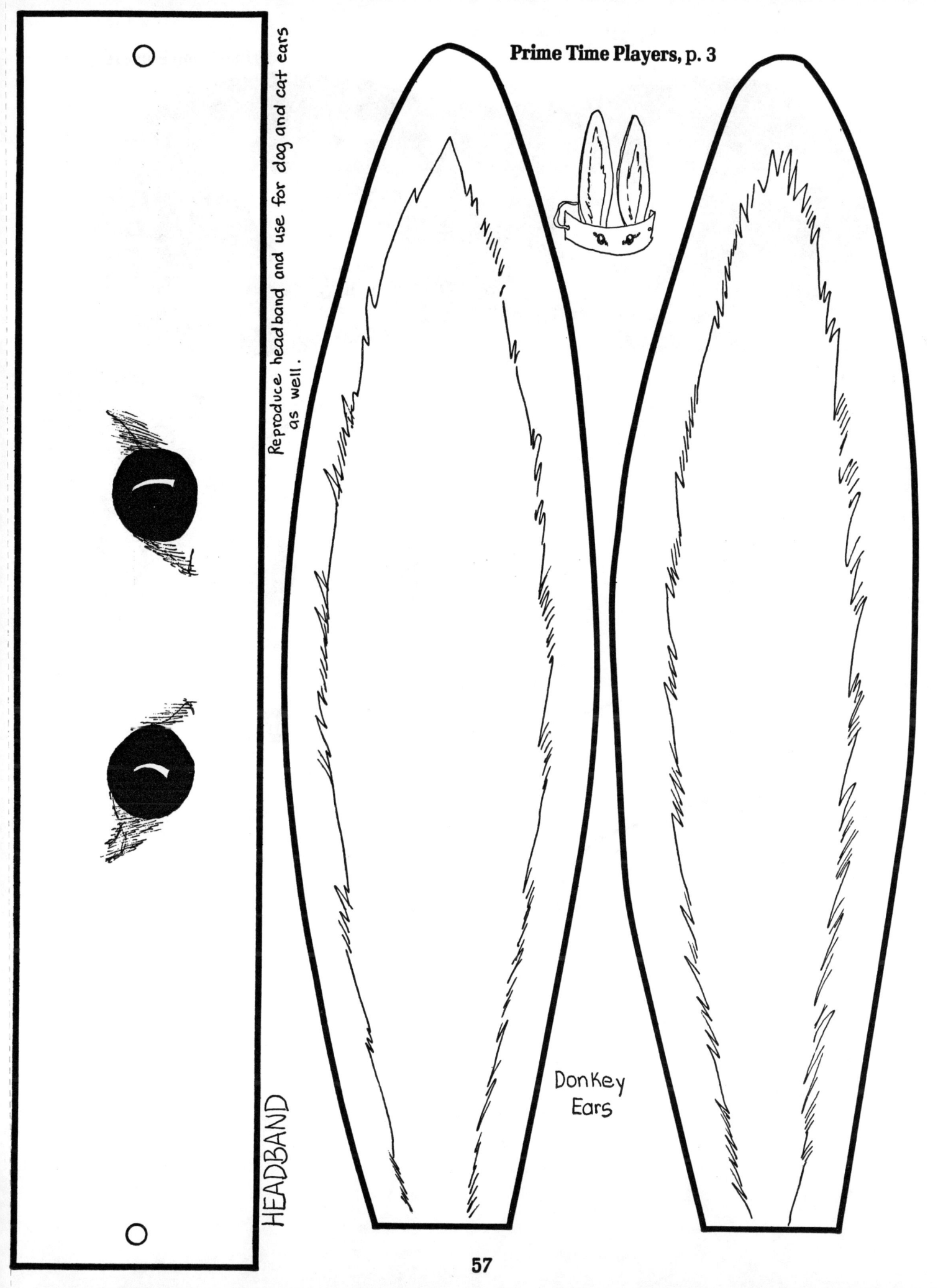

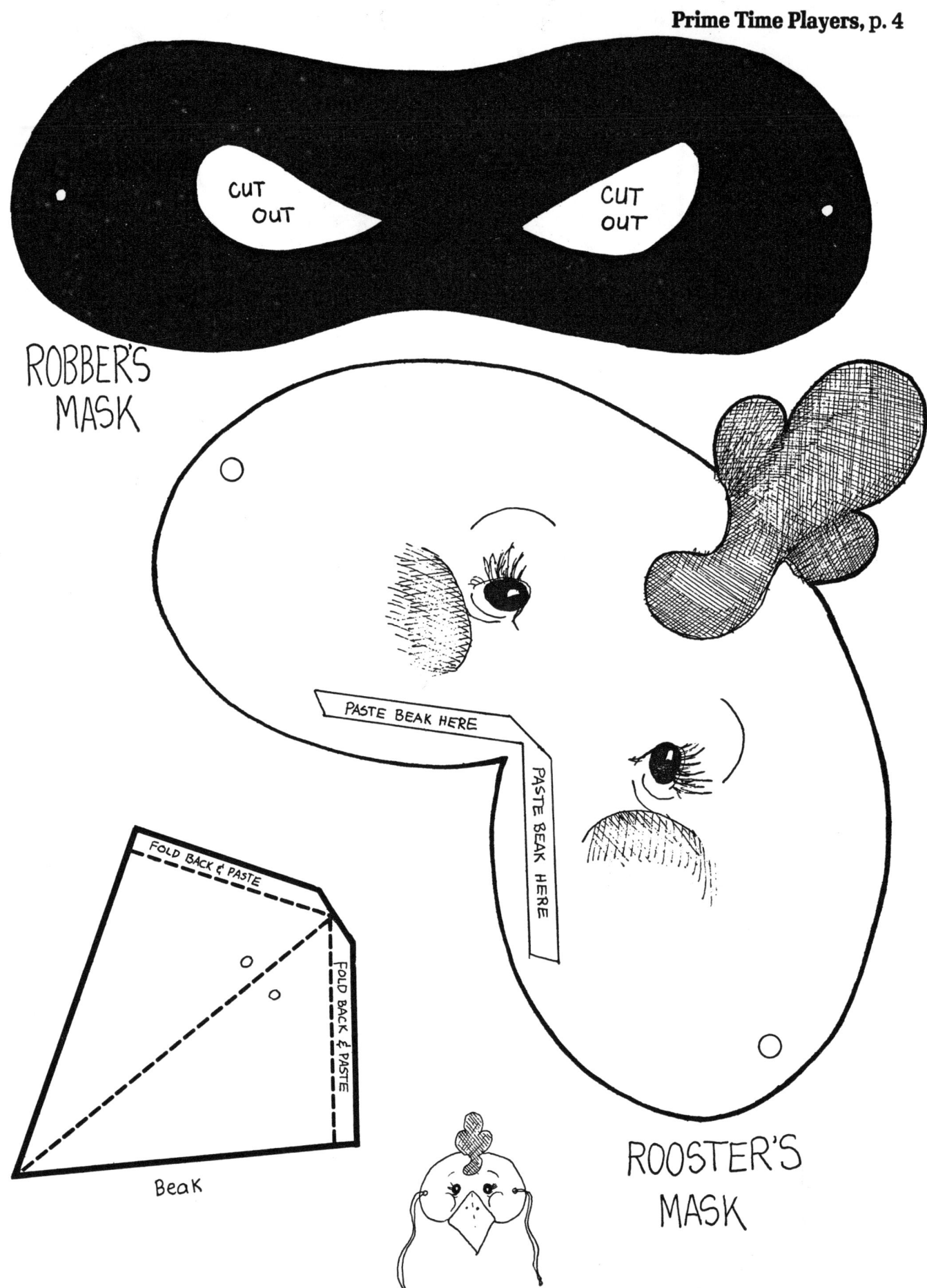

Prime Time Players, p. 5

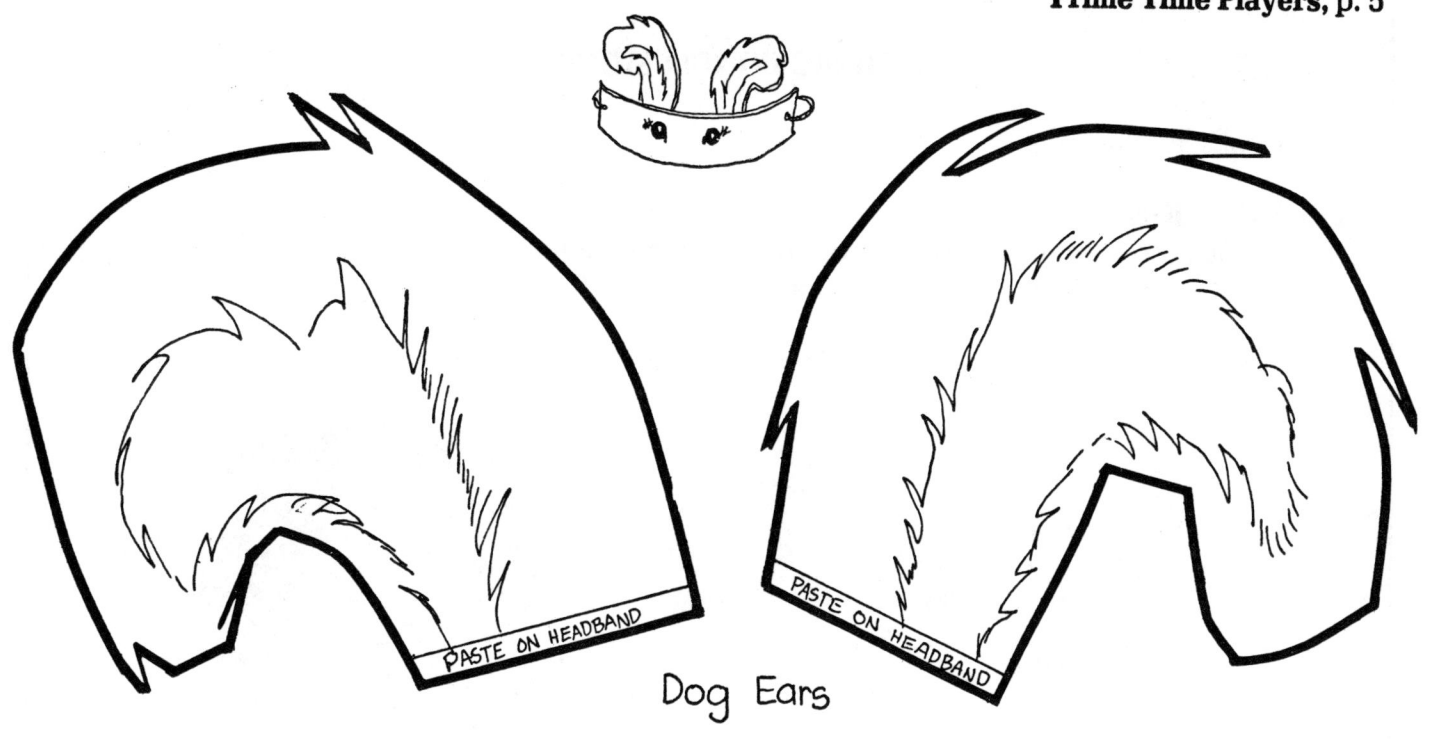

Dog Ears

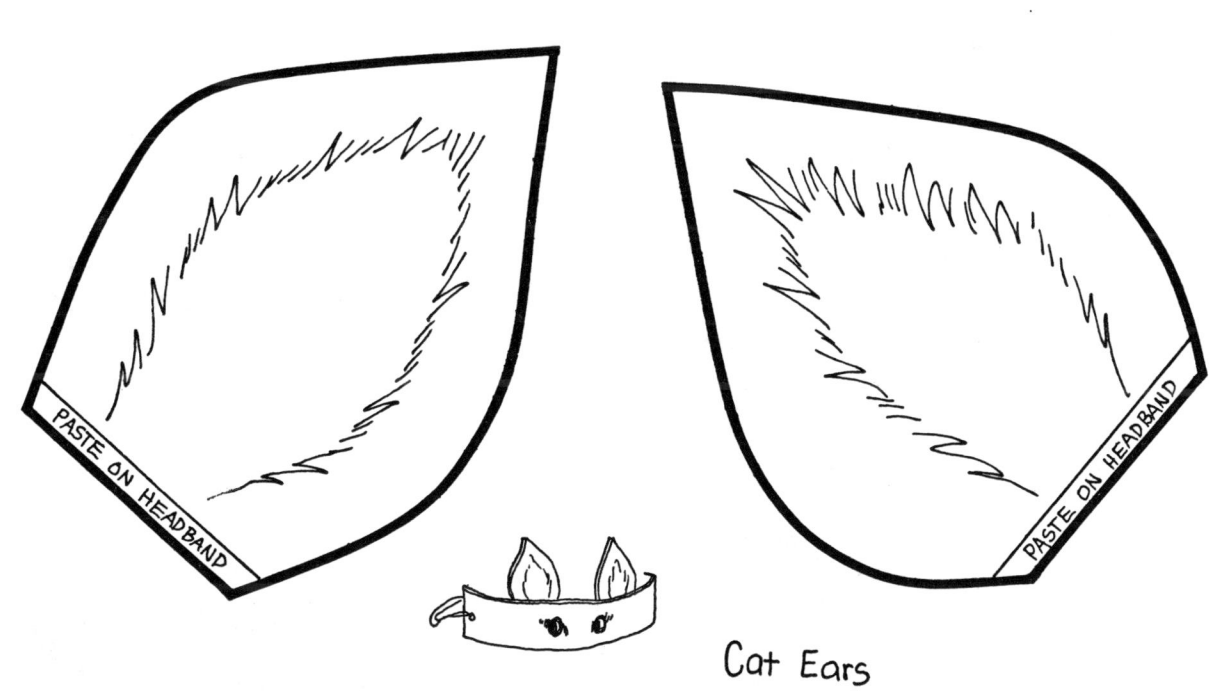

Cat Ears

COMIC CONCLUSIONS

PURPOSE: Sequencing

PREPARATION
1. Cut the same comic strip from the newspaper for two or three days. Be sure to use a strip that builds in sequence from day to day.

2. Paste the comic strips in a file folder, omitting one or more sections.

PROCEDURE
1. "Retelling a Story"—to show plot and sequence
   —Students write the story told in the comic strips in paragraph fashion, underlining the main idea, and being sure to include all the details. Remind the students that the pictures help to tell the story, so they must supply words to take the place of the pictures.

2. "Drawing Conclusions"
   —Provide paper and pencils for students to draw in the omitted sections.

3. "Who, When, Where and What"—
   —Students read the comic strip, and circle the "who," "when," "where" and "what" of the story. Be sure to provide students with erasable pencils so that other students will not receive clues from their work.

KRAZY KALEIDOSCOPE

Cut on the dotted lines and rearrange the pieces to solve this picture puzzle.

ROUND 'N WIGGLY

Hi! I'm Randy the Round Reptile. I like round things.
See if you can write the name of one thing that is round on each of my sections. Then, color me lightly and cut me out, around and around on the heavy black lines. Read your list of round things, and watch me wiggle!

WHERE DID THE TIME GO?

Keep a record of how you spend your out-of-school time for the next five days. At the end of the five days, you may be surprised to learn just where and how your time was spent.

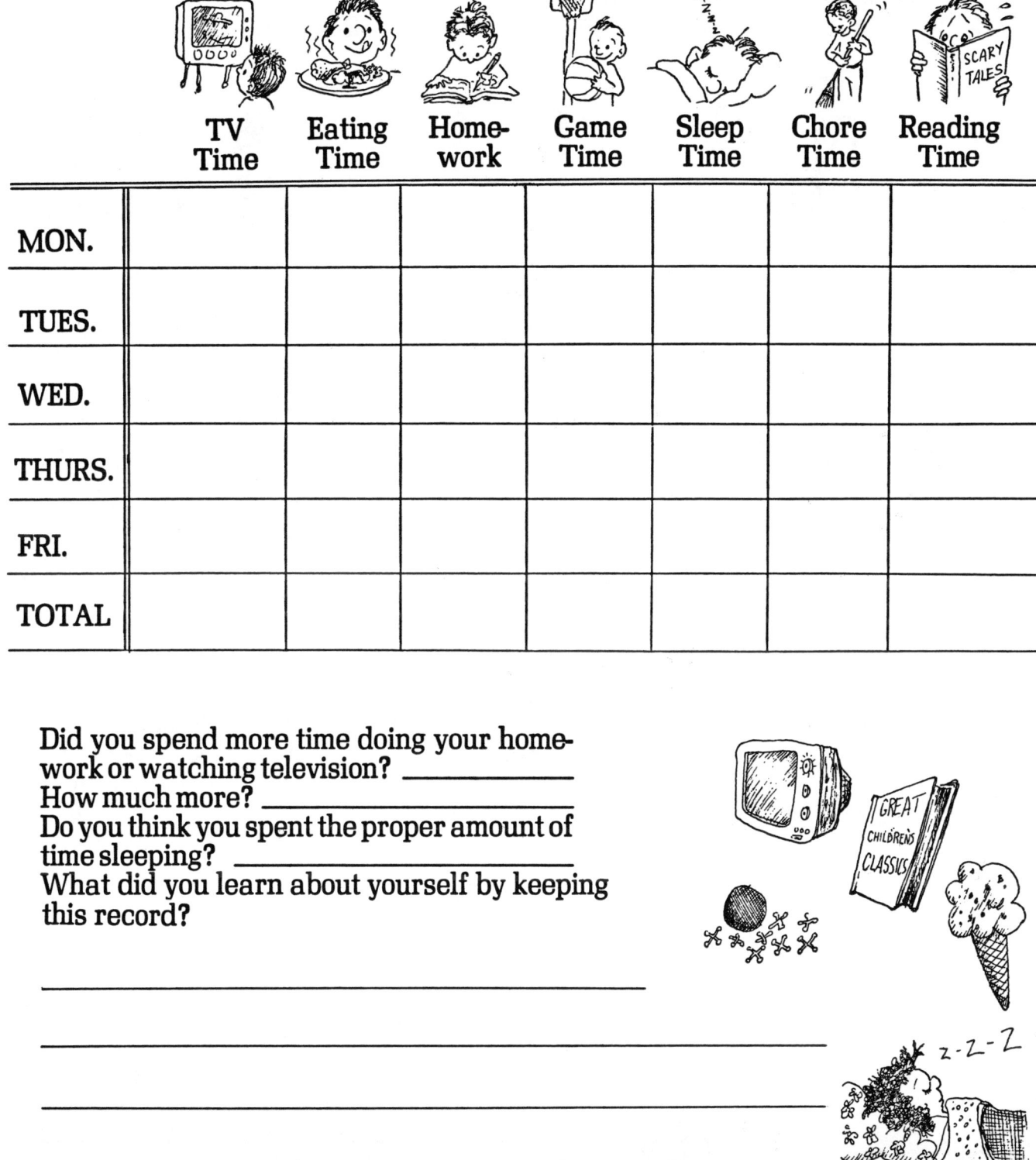

	TV Time	Eating Time	Home-work	Game Time	Sleep Time	Chore Time	Reading Time
MON.							
TUES.							
WED.							
THURS.							
FRI.							
TOTAL							

Did you spend more time doing your homework or watching television? _____
How much more? _____
Do you think you spent the proper amount of time sleeping? _____
What did you learn about yourself by keeping this record?

_____

_____

_____

_____

WATCH THE FINGERS!

Color and cut out the finger puppets. Choose one for each hand. Let these two puppets help you practice showing how you use your fingers to do one of the activities listed below.

When you and your puppets can do your activity perfectly, demonstrate it to the class. Be sure to have your puppets do the explaining!

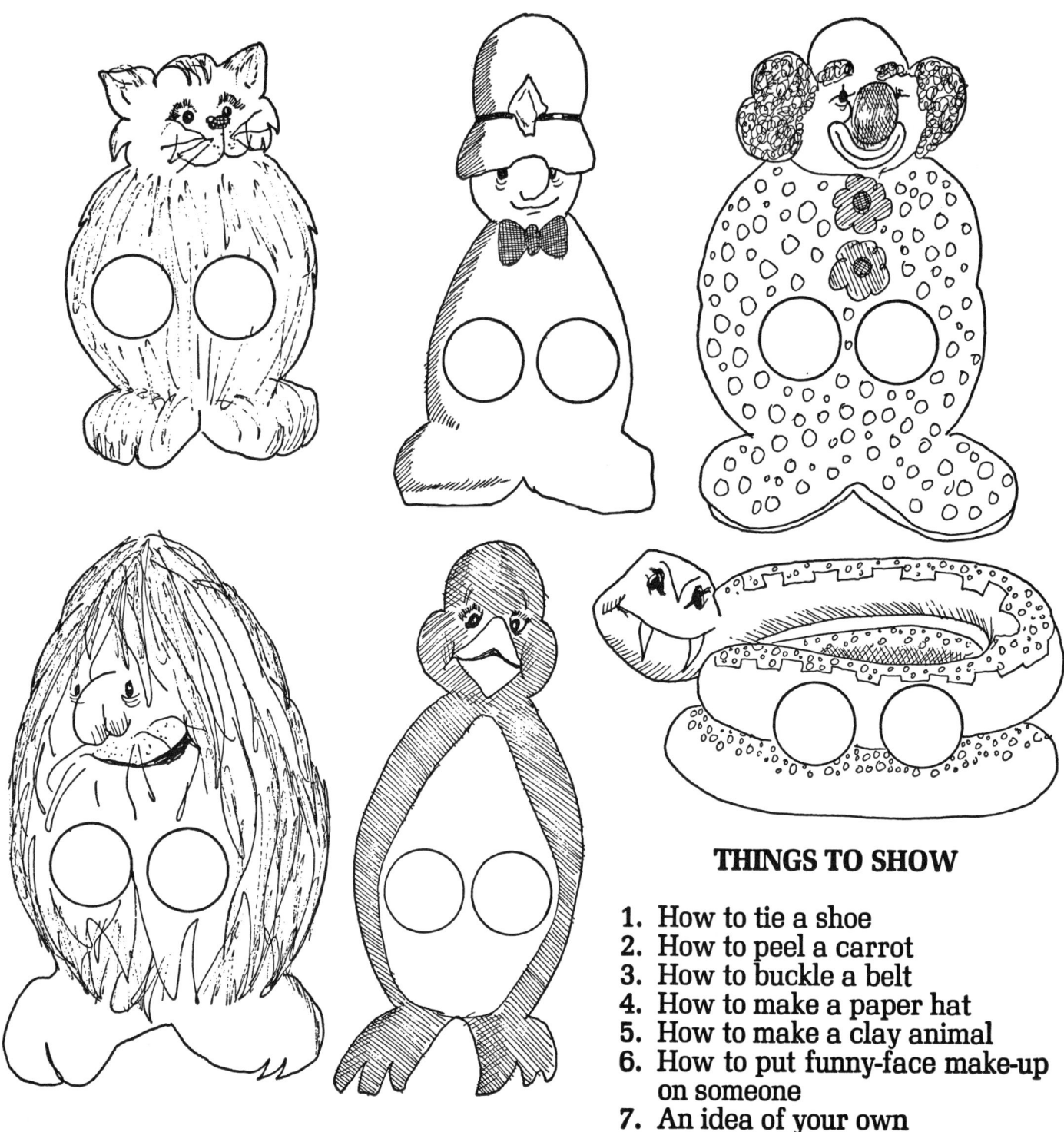

THINGS TO SHOW

1. How to tie a shoe
2. How to peel a carrot
3. How to buckle a belt
4. How to make a paper hat
5. How to make a clay animal
6. How to put funny-face make-up on someone
7. An idea of your own

FEELINGS ILLUSTRATED

Illustrate each of the feeling circles here. Use words or pictures in any way you wish. Try your hand at alliteration, an acrostic, haiku, a cinquain, a simile, drawings, or an idea all your own.

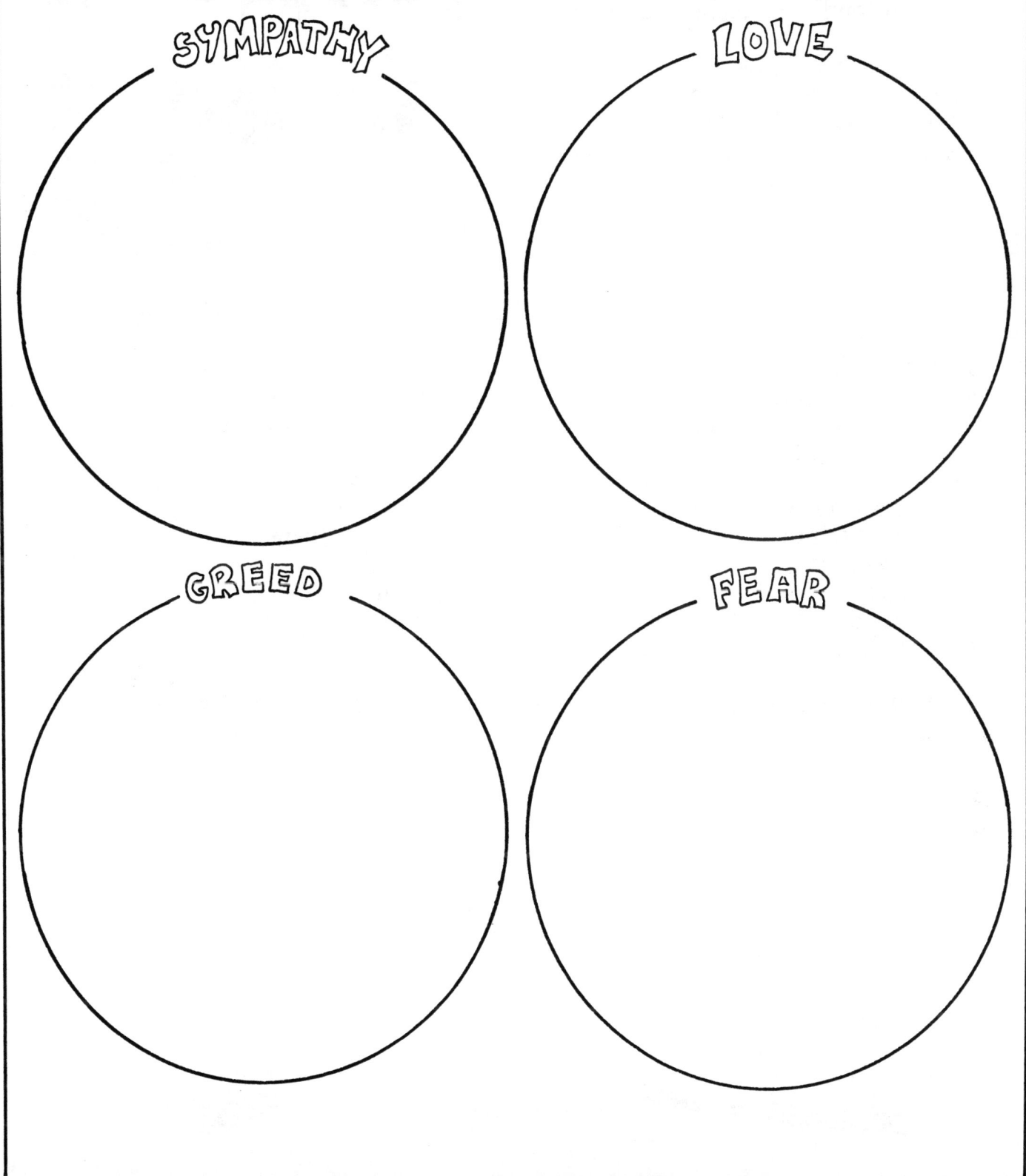

Gifted Giving

Choose a neighbor, a teacher, a best friend, or a family member for whom you would like to create a special gift.

Pretend that you have only the following materials available to you. Choose any 5 items on the list to use to create your special gift. Make a sketch of your proposed gift so you can get an idea of how it will look when it is finished.

- 1 box of whole cloves
- 3 jelly jars
- 1 yard of checkered gingham
- a basket of sea shells
- 6 spring-type clothespins
- 1 dozen oranges
- 12 yards of polka dot ribbon
- a tin cannister of loose tea
- 1 bottle of white glue
- 48 jumbo crayons
- a hammer
- 1 dozen nails in assorted sizes
- a loose-leaf notebook with a pack of lined paper
- 1 box of thumb tacks
- a ruler
- 2 small cardboard boxes
- a burlap bag full of peanuts
- 6-2' x 4' wooden boards
- a block of parrafin
- 12 sheets of multi-colored tissue paper
- 6 pecans
- scissors
- sewing thread
- needles
- 5 chocolate bars
- a hand saw
- 6 safety pins
- 1 package of 4" x 6" index cards
- 1 black, 1 red, 2 green, and 1 blue felt pens

Gifted Giving p. 2

Use this page to create a step-by-step diagram that shows the process you will use to create the gift. Draw each step in sequence so that someone else could follow the exact procedure to create a similar gift.

GIFTED GIVER'S DIAGRAM

A MAN'S A MAN FOR ALL THAT

There are many, many labels by which a man may be known. He may be a father, a banker, an artist, a friend, a critic, or a photographer.

Think of at least as many more labels for a man as there are spaces. If you can think of more, write them on the back.

LET'S FACE IT!

Add the kinds of features to each face that will make it show the emotion inferred by the quotation.

"Hey, you rascals! Get out of here!"

"Say, what's going on? Did I miss something?"

"Oh goody! I can't wait!"

"Ah, what a romantic evening."

"I just can't believe it!"

"But I'm so afraid I won't get the job!"

"Is this party for me?"

"Oh, no, I'm ruined!"

Write each word in this list near the one quotation that it best fits.

bewilderment   amazement   dejection   despair
anticipation   surprise   fantasy   anger

ROCK CRITTERS

Make a rock critter for a special gift for someone you like a lot. You will need some small rocks, glue, and acrylic paint.

What to Do
1. Look for interestingly shaped rocks that will "go together" to make a rock critter.

2. Play around with the rocks until you get an insect or an animal that really sends you. A lady bug, a fat pig, a turtle, or a bug-eyed creature from another planet might be fun. Don't settle for the first and easiest creation you put together. Continue experimenting with different arrangements until you have something entirely original.

3. Glue the rocks together, and let them dry. Then paint on faces or other interesting features.

BOY-OH-BOY, BUBBLES!

PURPOSE: Experimenting and Recording

PREPARATION
1. Gather the following materials.

   liquid detergent
   glycerin (small size)
   plastic drinking straws
   paper towels
   pie pans
   several 12" lengths of insulated wire

2. Place all materials in a center accessible to students.

3. Prepare some of both "Bubble" recipes. Attach a copy of each recipe to its container so that students may read recipes.

4. Provide a copy of the following activity page for each student.

PROCEDURE
1. Introduce the "Bubble" activity center to the students. Direct students to follow the instructions and suggestions on the activity page to make their own discoveries about bubbles.

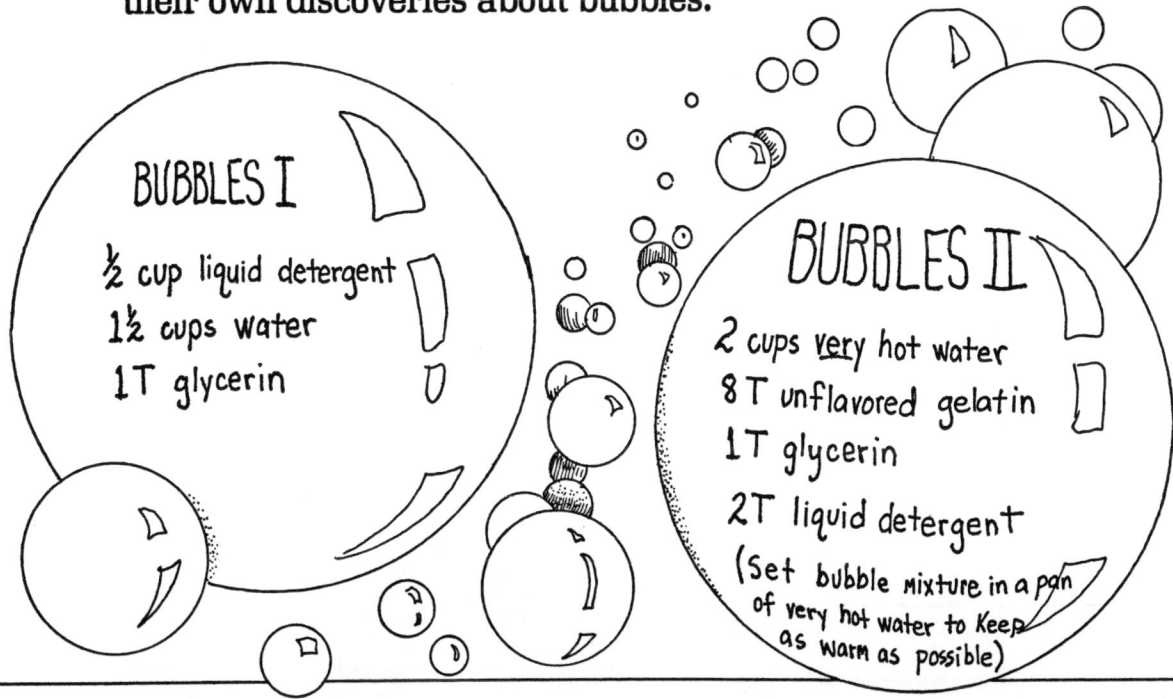

BUBBLES I
½ cup liquid detergent
1½ cups water
1T glycerin

BUBBLES II
2 cups very hot water
8T unflavored gelatin
1T glycerin
2T liquid detergent
(Set bubble mixture in a pan of very hot water to keep as warm as possible)

Boy-Oh-Boy, Bubbles!

What do you know about bubbles? Use the materials in the "Bubbles" center to complete these experiments.

First, read the recipes for "Bubbles I" and "Bubbles II."

USING "BUBBLES I"

1. Bend a piece of insulated wire to make a wire ring at one end. Use it as a bubble "wand." Then, choose a drinking straw for blowing bubbles. Try both of these methods for making bubbles. Which method makes the best bubbles for you?
   _____

   Which is more fun for you to use?
   _____

2. Using any method you choose, try these:

   A. Make as large a bubble as you can. About how large is it in diameter?
      _____

   B. How many bubbles can you make with one blow through the straw?
      _____

   C. How many bubbles can you make with one wand full of bubble mix?
      _____

   D. Is there any way to enlarge a bubble once it has become detached from the straw?
      _____
      _____
      _____
      _____

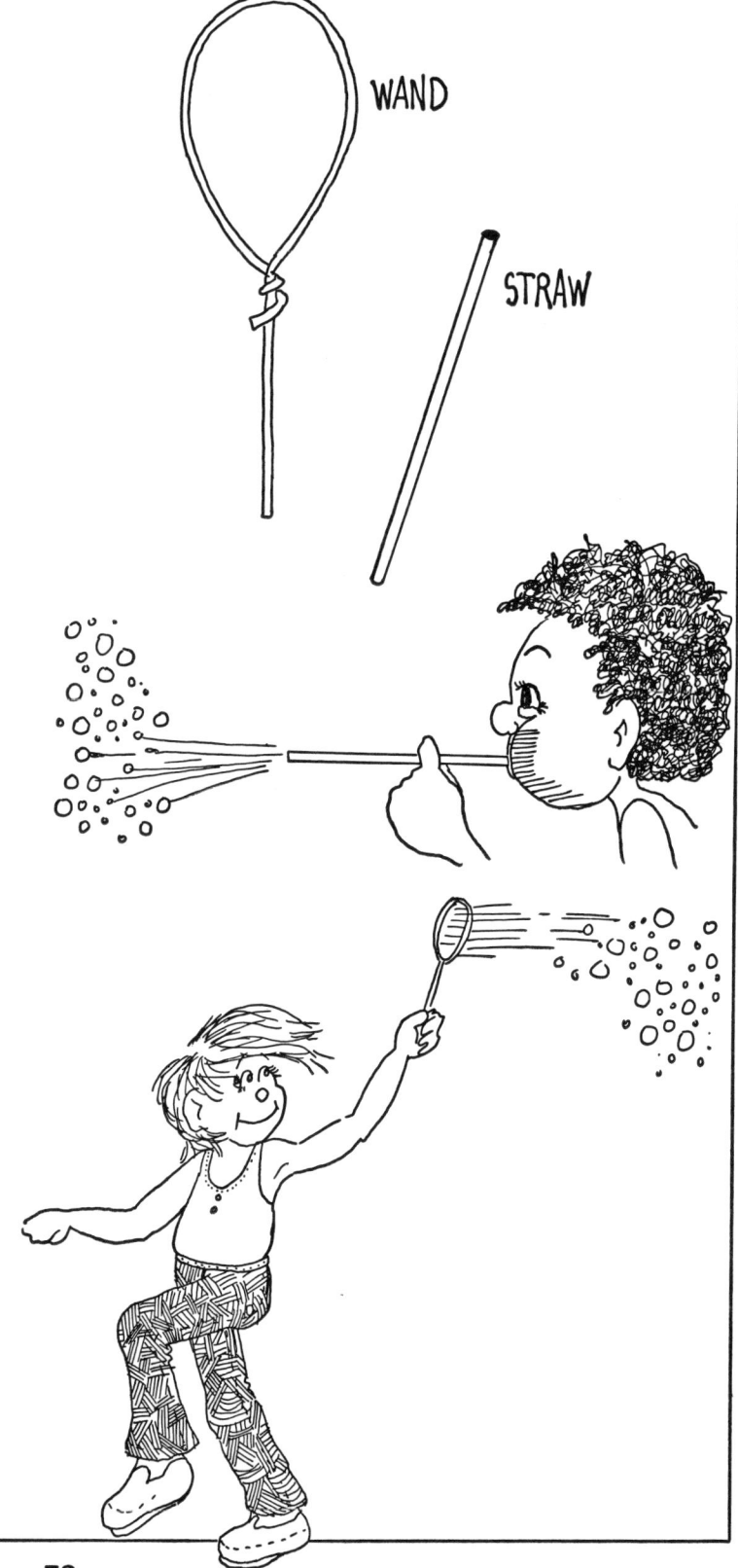

72

Boy-Oh-Boy, Bubbles!

USING "BUBBLES II"

1. Try to make these bubble shapes.

   Bubble Bouquet

   A Double Bubble
   (one inside the other)

   Bubble Pyramid

2. Which is the best suds recipe to use, "Bubbles I" or "Bubbles II"?

JUST FOR FUN

1. Try to make some unusual "Bubble Catchers."

2. Experiment with dividing bubbles.

3. Stretch bubbles to make crazy shapes.

4. Draw a fantasy "Bubble Sculpture" on another sheet of paper. Then, try to create it with real bubbles.

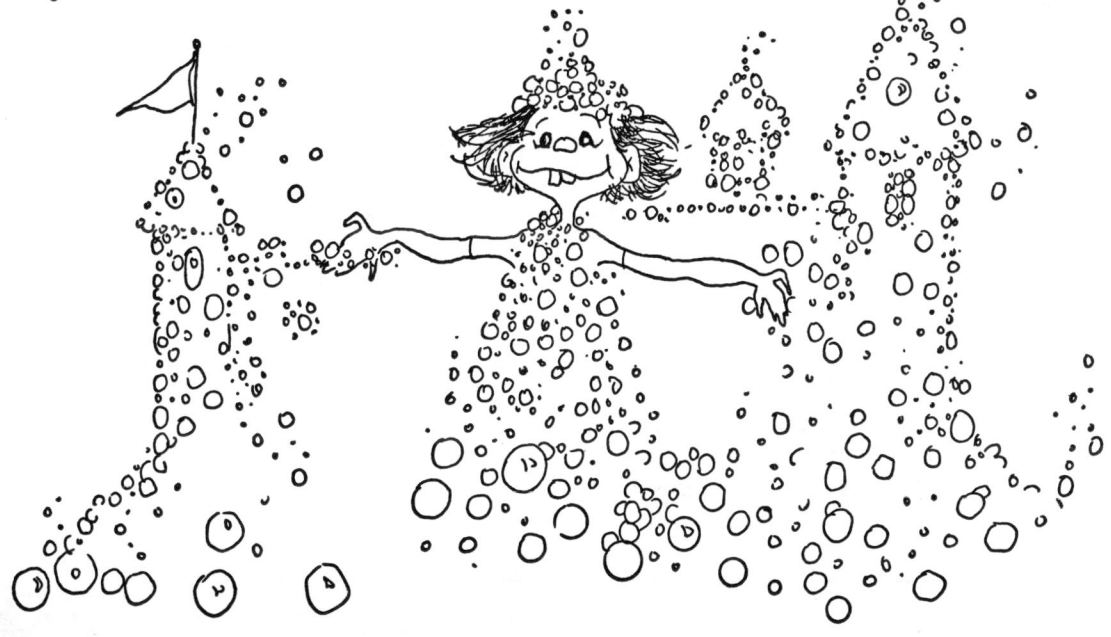

PICTURE THIS

Select one of the free verse poems below to finish creatively in only two lines. Draw and color a picture on a separate sheet of paper to illustrate your completed poem. Don't forget to put yourself both in the ending and in the picture.

Flat on my back, I lie
    on a grassy hillside on a clear, sunny day.
      The sky is blue, blue.
      The clouds go floating by . . .
As I lie here half asleep, I think of

_____

and_____

Imagine, if you can, this beautiful tropical isle with lush green trees,
    magenta blossoms,
    azure seas
      and
    golden sunsets.
I can think of no more perfect way to end the
    day than with this

_____

and_____

Suddenly the clouds darkened,
    the winds began to howl
      and the ocean to roar.
Where to go for shelter?
How to protect myself from the storm?
    These were my only thoughts.
Just as the sky seemed to explode, I

_____

_____

Survival Scheme

PURPOSE: Surviving/Multi-Skill

PREPARATION

1. Set up the learning center in a spot easily accessible to the group.

2. Prepare the "Great Inventions" box and study guide (see activity) and a "Great Inventions" bulletin board.

3. Reproduce the pupil activity pages and add these to the center.

4. Provide paper, pencils, crayons, and other art supplies.

PROCEDURE

1. Arrange time and space for students to complete the center activites.

Survival Scheme Center

LOST!

You are lost in the woods with three friends your own age. You are surrounded by huge trees, and no path leads in or out. The sun has set, and the forest is growing cold and dark. You have only left-overs from your picnic lunch, half a thermos of water, light sweaters, and empty back packs.

One of your friends suggests that you should all go in different directions for a short distance looking for a path to follow out of the woods, and then return to the spot where you are now and leave the forest together.

Another member of the group feels very strongly that, since it is nearly dark, the best thing to do is to settle in for the night and wait until morning to try to find the way home.

The third friend has no ideas to offer.

Think about each of the proposed solutions. Consider the strengths and weaknesses of each, and make a check beside the one you consider best. Tell why you selected it.

_____

_____

_____

_____

_____

_____

_____

_____

_____

Survival Scheme Center

Presenting A Plan

Rethink the proposed solutions and decide upon a plan of your own. Your plan may or may not include some portion of one or both of the other two.

Use a formal outline to explain your plan so that your friends will understand and accept it.

MY PLAN

Survival Scheme Center

SELECTION LIMITED

Select the three items you think would be most helpful to the four lost people. Circle the items. In the inner circle, write three sentences to explain why you selected these items and how they would be used.

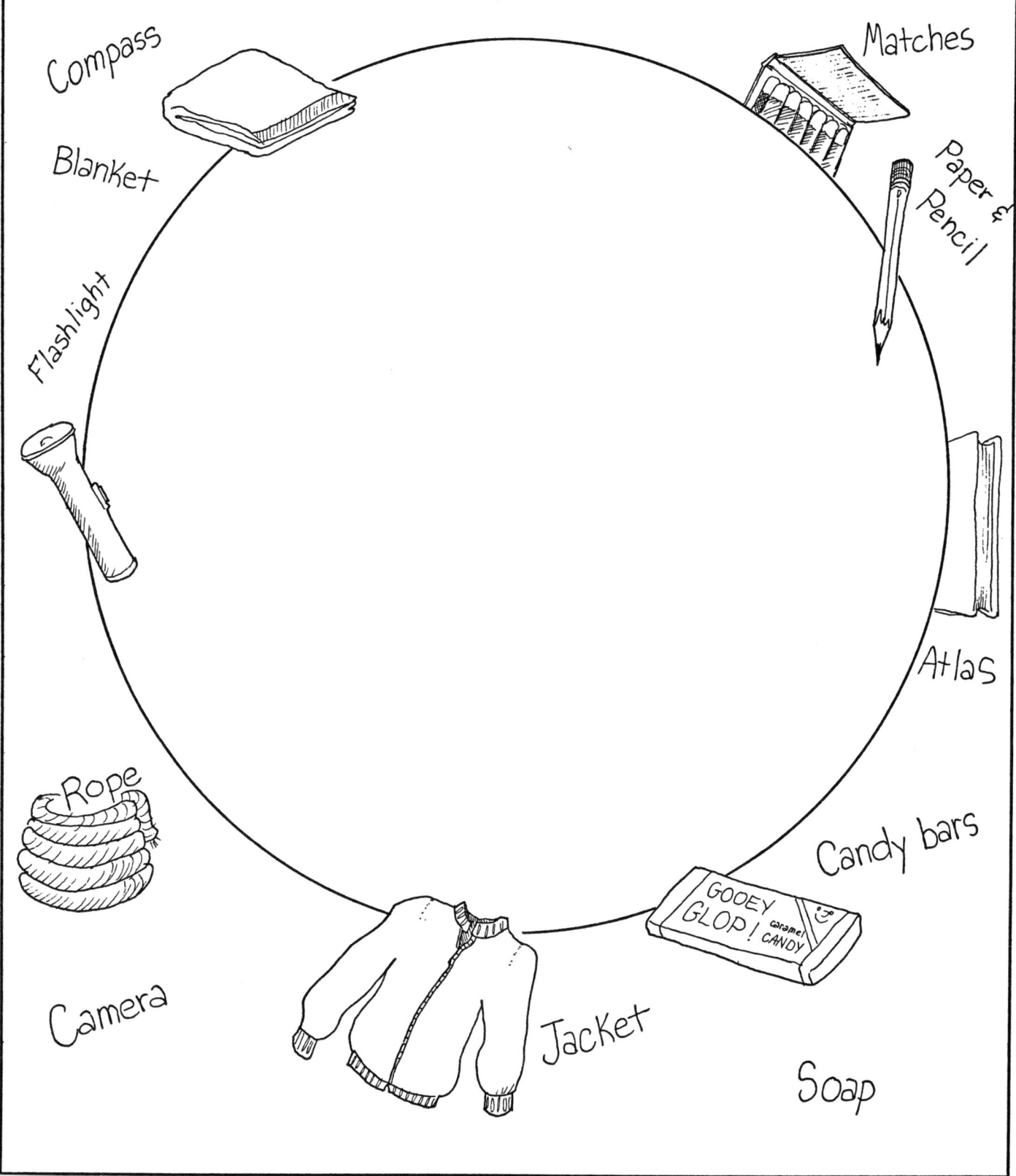

78

EMOTION INVENTORY

Because you and your friends are faced with a frightening situation and have a difficult choice to make, you will experience various emotions and feelings within a very brief time period.

Circle the emotions and feelings that you would expect to be experienced by some or all members of the group.

ANGER SYMPATHY COURAGE

GRIEF JOY

FEAR

HAPPINESS

GENEROSITY

GREED

PATIENCE

HOSTILITY

ANXIETY

EXCITEMENT FRIENDSHIP LOVE

AGGRESSIVENESS

Role Relationships

PURPOSE: Dramatizing

PREPARATION
1. Arrange a time and place for students to work in groups of four to role play the situation given in "Lost!" Discuss the problem, the proposed solutions, and the character implications before groups begin role playing.

   For example: One friend **suggested** a plan, another **felt very strongly**, a third had **absolutely no ideas** or suggestions, and the fourth **presented a detailed outline**. How do you bring this out in role playing?

   Is the problem agreeing upon a plan, sticking together, getting out of the forest, or something else? Is it easy to stick to the main topic in role playing?

   How does it feel to be in the person's shoes you will be representing? Can you really "feel" and "act" with and for that person?

PROCEDURE
1. Allow ample time for each group to gain the full benefit of the role playing situation.

2. Gather the total group for an evaluation discussion. Focus on questions such as these.
   - What emotions surfaced during the role playing?
   - How did it feel to be the person with no ideas to share?
   - Did some solutions to the real problem emerge?

3. Wrap up the discussion with an analysis of role playing as a vehicle for creative thinking.

A PERSONAL EXPERIENCE

Write a paragraph about a personal experience of yours (real or imaginary) that required the use of good survival skills.

We ran out of gas on the freeway, on the way to Grandma's house. Dad had to walk to the gas station, and I was left alone in the car.

Survival Scheme Center

GREAT INVENTIONS

PURPOSE: Assembling

PREPARATION
1. Provide a big box of good junk containing these and other materials.

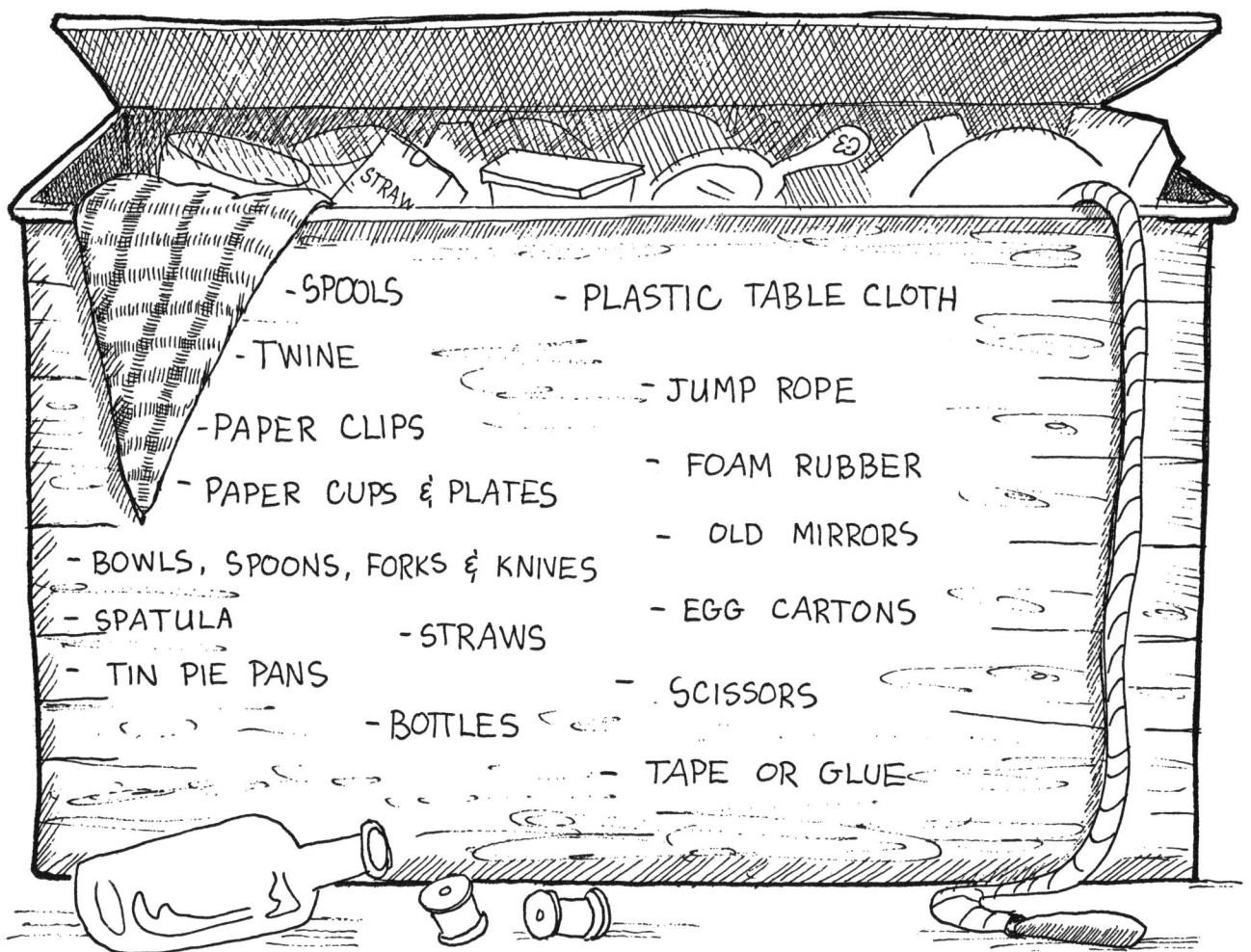

- SPOOLS
- TWINE
- PAPER CLIPS
- PAPER CUPS & PLATES
- BOWLS, SPOONS, FORKS & KNIVES
- SPATULA
- TIN PIE PANS
- STRAWS
- BOTTLES
- PLASTIC TABLE CLOTH
- JUMP ROPE
- FOAM RUBBER
- OLD MIRRORS
- EGG CARTONS
- SCISSORS
- TAPE OR GLUE

2. Print the following directions on a study guide and place it beside the box.

PROCEDURE

"Great Inventions"

1. Use materials from this box to assemble an item to help you find your way out of the forest.

2. Draw a diagram of the completed item, give it a name, and write a description of it.

3. Add your completed diagram and description to the "Great Inventions" bulletin board.

It's a Kid's Life

"How do you think life for kids today compares with life for your parents when they were kids? Is it easier or harder? In what ways?"

Those are tough questions to answer, aren't they?

Interview six of your classmates to find out what they think about it. Use a separate sheet of paper to make notes for each interview. Add your own opinion, and tabulate the results.

Summarize your findings here as clearly and concisely as possible.

_____
_____
_____
_____
_____
_____
_____
_____
_____
_____
_____
_____
_____
_____

SHIPWRECKED!

Pretend you have been shipwrecked on a small tropical island. Another one of the survivors is a small girl who lost her very favorite toy—a doll house—in the shipwreck. You want to make her happy by creating a temporary doll house for her to play with on the island.

The little girl has started a list of the things her new house will need. Your job is to find materials to use and ways to put them together to simulate each piece.

Choose the 2 pieces you will make first. Draw a picture of how each will look when it is finished. Then, add labels to the picture to tell what materials you used and where you found them.

2 BEDS
1 TABLE
1 CUPBOARD
1 STOVE
1 BATHTUB
1 LAMP
1 CLOCK

EX.: Plan for Sink

- sea shell
- piece of driftwood found on beach
- small block of wood from ship

Use the clues on the following page to complete this crosswood puzzle. You have been given only one hint—the space where #2 starts. Can you complete the puzzle?

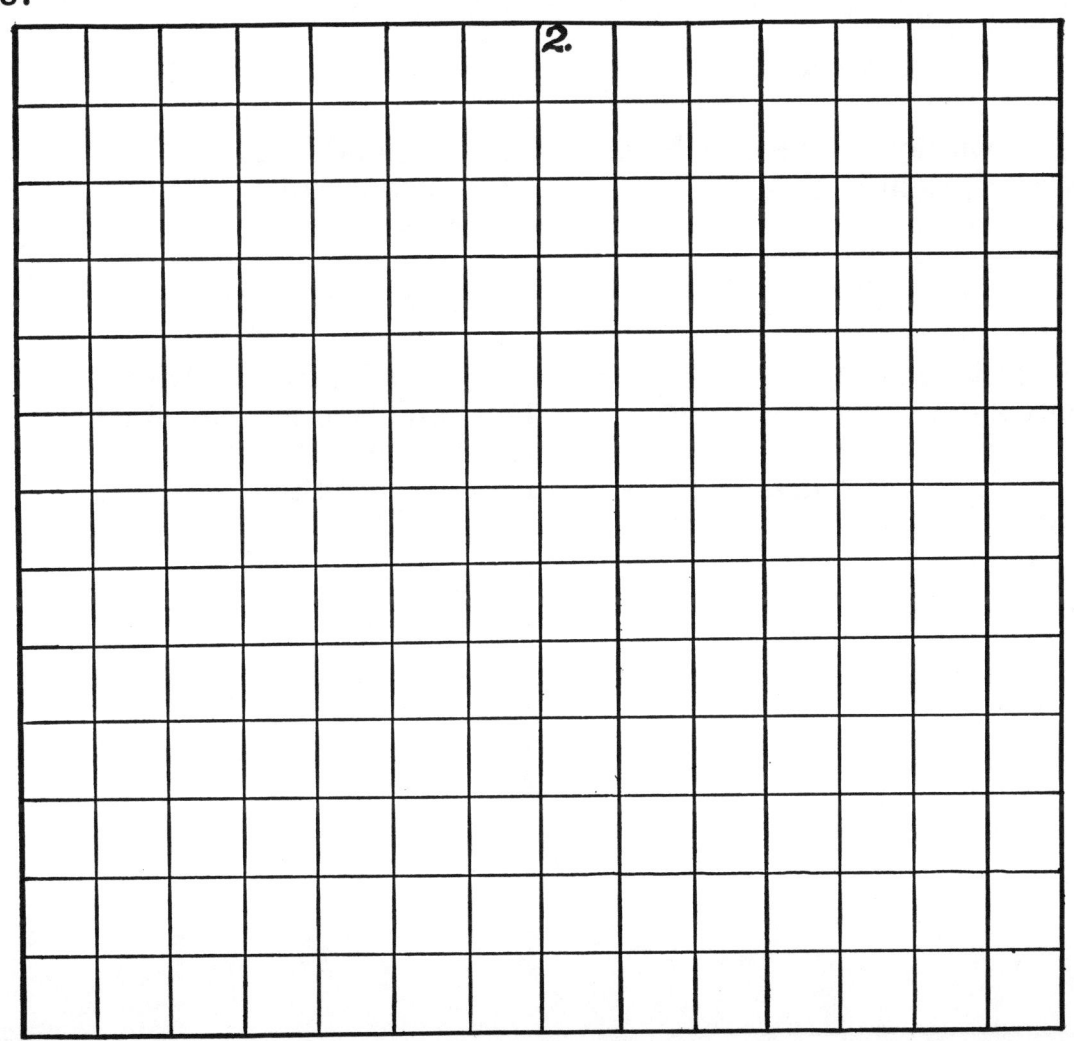

A Sight for Crossed Eyes

ACROSS

2. Abbreviation for Miss or Mrs.
5. Braniff, Delta, TWA, Air Canada
8. Not succeed
9. Expert combat flyer
10. Opposite of "she"
11. Negative answer
13. Between Lamentations and Daniel
14. Herb-flavored sparkling drink
15. Short for Edward
16. Law degree
18. Purify
21. Black gold
22. A pointed beard
26. Not high
28. Greeting
30. Holy messenger
32. Affirm

DOWN

1. ___ and Mrs.
2. Famous Italian painter
3. Achoo!
4. Fence
5. Story with a moral
6. Sol, ___ te, do
7. Garment for mourning
11. Can't find in a haystack
12. No longer young
17. Prevaricate
19. Nimble
20. A, ___, I, ___ U
23. A continent
24. Skilled
25. Feminine for "he"
27. Past tense of "is"
29. For example (abbreviation)
31. Green light says, "___."

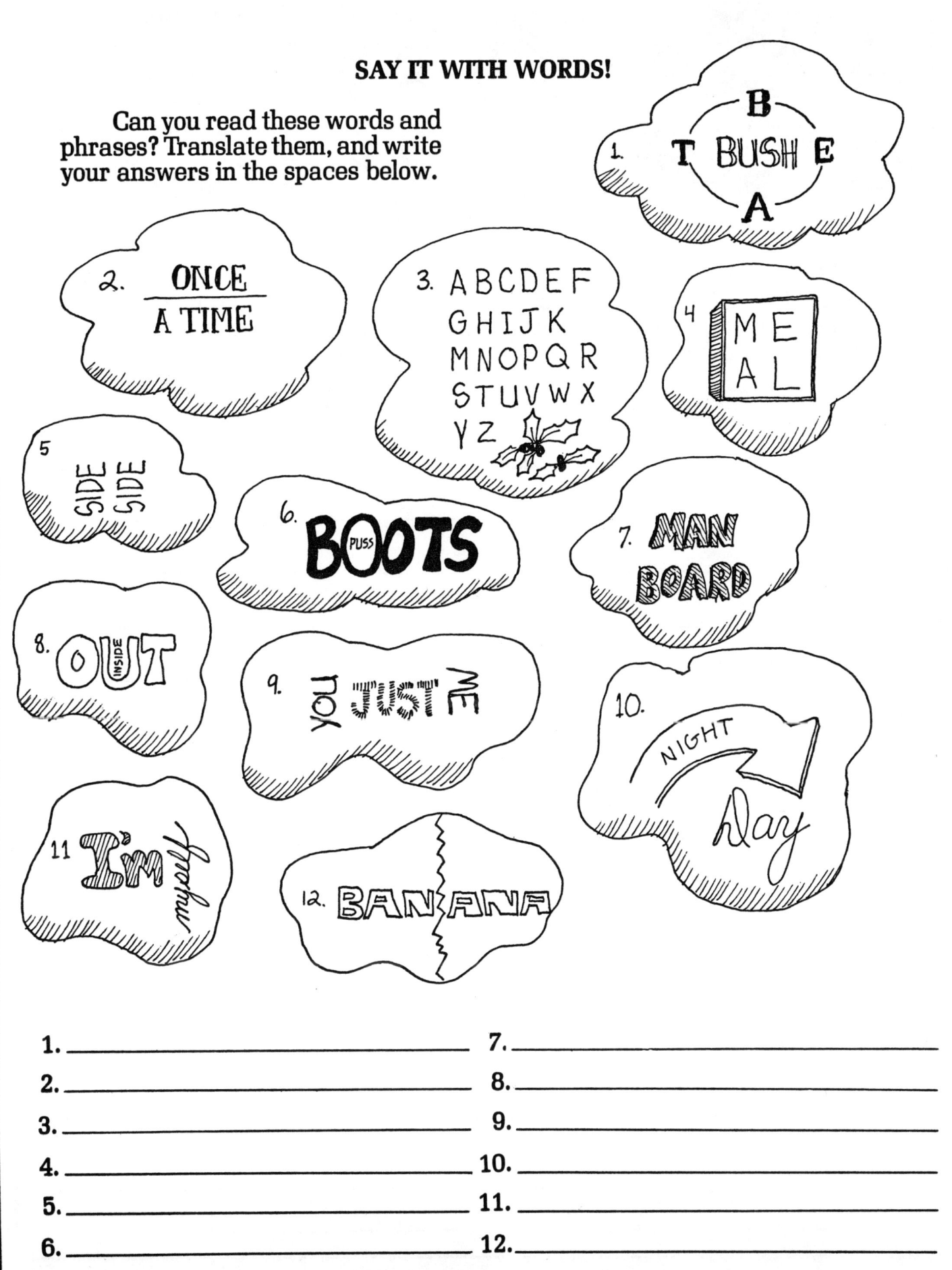

A Tour Too Good To Miss!

This is your big chance to find out how good you would be as a tour director. Plan a full day sight-seeing tour of your own city. Do your research—remember to include all the important sights you want visitors to see, and still leave time for a fun lunch and rest breaks.

Places to Visit	What to See
_____	_____
_____	_____
_____	_____
_____	_____
_____	_____
_____	_____
_____	_____
_____	_____
_____	_____
_____	_____

Method of transportation: _____ Cost of tour: _____
Other Notes: _____
_____   _____
_____   _____

A Tour Too Good To Miss

Fill in your tour schedule here.

8:00 a.m.—Coffee, hot chocolate, and tour overview

8:30 a.m.— _____

9:00 a.m.— _____

9:30 a.m.— _____

10:00 a.m.— _____

10:30 a.m.— _____

11:00 a.m.— _____

11:30 a.m.— _____

12:00 noon— _____

12:30 p.m.— _____

1:00 p.m.— _____

1:30 p.m.— _____

2:00 p.m.— _____

2:30 p.m.— _____

3:00 p.m.— _____

3:30 p.m.— _____

4:00 p.m.—Tour ends—Farewell and Happy Memories

A Tour Too Good To Miss

LET ME TELL YOU...

Getting off to a good start can make all the difference in how a tour day goes.

People want to know from the very beginning where they are going and why. Write the explanation for your tour here. When you finish, check to make sure your explanation is both colorful and informative.

THE REPORTERS' REPORTER

We usually think of reporters as news people—people that find and report on stories for television or radio stations, or for newspapers. But reporting is actually a part of many other jobs, too.

Pretend that you are a Reporters' Reporter. Your assignment is to report on the kinds of reporters and the subjects of the reports they might make in the working situations given below.

A Report on Reporters

Location	Reporter	Subject of Report
1. SCHOOL	attendance officer	attendance information
	teacher	progress reports for file
	cafeteria supervisor	amounts of food used / amount of $ needed for food
2. OFFICE		
3. DEPARTMENT STORE		
4. STREET CORNER		
5. POLICE OR FIRE STATION		

The Reporters' Reporter, p. 2

Location	Reporter	Subject of Report
6. SHIP		
7. AIRPORT		
8. GARAGE		
9. HOME		
10. WAREHOUSE		
11. FACTORY		
12. HOSPITAL		

APPLICATION COMPETENCY REVIEW

1. Look at the first two sets of numbers below. Then, circle the set of numbers that would most logically follow those sets.

   2-4-6-7; 3-5-7-8; _____?_____

   5-7-9-10   4-6-8-9   4-6-7-8

2. Circle the letter beside the example (or examples) below that demonstrates the process of listing.

   | A. | 3 dolls
5 balls
6 planes
7 trucks
4 bats
+ 1 yo yo
26 toys | B. | Do you
know
that only
very or-
ganized
people
make
lists? | C. | apples
peaches
bananas
grapes
oranges
lemons
plums | D. | What
time
do you
leave
home
to get
there? |

3. Read the paragraph and study the diagram below. Then, circle the numbers on the diagram that show the places at which Casey the Cat stopped during his midnight travels around the town.

   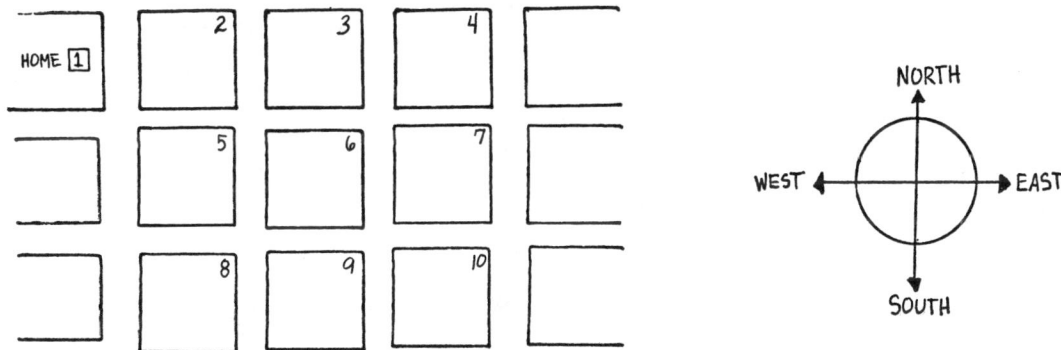

   Casey left the house at midnight. He traveled ½ block south and then 2 blocks east, and stopped near a large tree on the right. From high in the tree, an owl watched him turn south and travel to a garbage can 1 block away on the right. Then, Casey made his way east 1 block, turned north, and came to rest near a bush 2 blocks away on the left. From there, he turned west and ran 3 blocks and then ½ block south to his home.

4. Draw a circle around the letter beside the question below that the owl in question #3 would be most likely to answer correctly.

   A. How many blocks did Casey travel from the tree to the garbage can?
   B. Why was Casey out traveling?
   C. Was Casey a large cat or a small cat?

5. Draw a circle around the letter below that most accurately describes the diagram in question #3.

   A. a simulation of a neighborhood
   B. a schedule of a cat's night out
   C. an outline of a trip

6. Beside each face, write the number of the word that tells which emotion it shows.

   1. anger
   2. surprise
   3. sorrow
   4. apathy

7. Draw a circle around the word below that is least likely to be associated with the word fly.

   wall   baseball
   plane   swat

8. Arrange the words below in the puzzle squares so that they all fit together and each still maintains its own identity.

   BUY
   BOB
   TRY
   BUT

9. Put a check beside the statement below that is the most accurate interpretation of this rebus message.

   ___ Act like an animal.
   ___ Behave nicely.
   ___ Eat heartily.

10. Put a check beside the statement below that is an explanation of the addition process.

    ___ joining one group of items to another group of items to obtain a total number of items
    ___ counting two groups of items
    ___ the opposite of subtracting items from a group

11. Draw a circle around the adjective below which best describes a fire which is burning out of control.

    huge   raging
    dazzling   excruciating

12. Present the information given in the following sentence in outline form.

    Affectionate, dependent, demanding, often wet, and always hungry are characteristics that describe babies.

NOTE: Many of the skills and processes presented in this section are best evaluated by more open-ended experiences than can be provided in a written competency review format. It is suggested that the teacher use the glossary as a guide to create additional evaluative activities similar to the models in the text.

SKILLSTUFF

ANALYSIS

III. ANALYSIS SKILLS AND PROCESSES　　　　　　　SKILLSTUFF Activities

___ Categorizing

___ Inventorying

___ Calculating

___ Separating

___ Solving

___ Dissecting

___ Relating

___ Differentiating

___ Comparing/Contrasting

___ Surveying

___ Abstracting

___ Advertising

___ Decoding

___ Generalizing

A PACKING PROBLEM

After months of planning, the Martins are ready to pack the car for their vacation trip. Even the baby brother is wide awake and ready to go! Sue Ann and Barbara offered to put everything except the personal bags in the trunk of the car, but somehow, they just never expected to have so many different things to get into the three boxes that will fit in the trunk.

Mr. Smithson, their favorite neighbor, came out to say good-bye and to offer his help. He suggested that they arrange all the items by categories and label the boxes so they will be easier to unpack when they arrive at the ski lodge.

Help the girls get organized by drawing circles around all the food, squares around all recreation and hobby equipment, and triangles around the clothing.

A Packing Problem, p. 2

Write the name of each item in the correct box. Use your dictionary if you need spelling help.

DO YOU REMEMBER!

Test your reading comprehension skills without rereading "A Packing Problem." Read the statements below. Decide whether each statement is true or false, and show your decision by circling the figure in the appropriate column beside it.

After you have completed the test, reread the story and write under each statement the sentence from the story that proves your answer right or wrong. Give yourself 5 points for each correct answer.

True   False

1. The vacation trip came as a pleasant surprise for the Martin family.

2. Sue Ann and Barbara offered to do all the family packing.

3. Everything had to be sorted and packed in three boxes.

4. The helpful neighbor's name is Mr. Smith.

5. The Martins are excited about this trip to the beach.

6. Sue Ann and Barbara have a baby brother.

CLASSIFICATION CLARIFICATION

PURPOSE: Categorizing

PREPARATION
1. Assemble a collection of many colors of buttons in a sturdy box (a shoe box or a cookie tin will work well).

2. Provide a tray for sorting.

PROCEDURE
1. Direct students who need additional concrete experience to sort the buttons by color or by size.

ALTERNATE ACTIVITY

Cut pictures of fruits and vegetables from magazines or seed catalogs. Paste them on white index cards and write "fruit" or "vegetable" on the back of each. Print the following directions on the front of a sturdy envelope, and place the cards inside.

"Put the fruits in one stack and the vegetables in another. When you have finished, turn the cards over to check your classification skills."

100

CLOSED FOR INVENTORY

Pretend that you are the owner of a store called "Topsy-Turvy Toyland." It is time for you to make your inventory—to find out exactly what you have in your store.

Use this inventory sheet to check your stock.

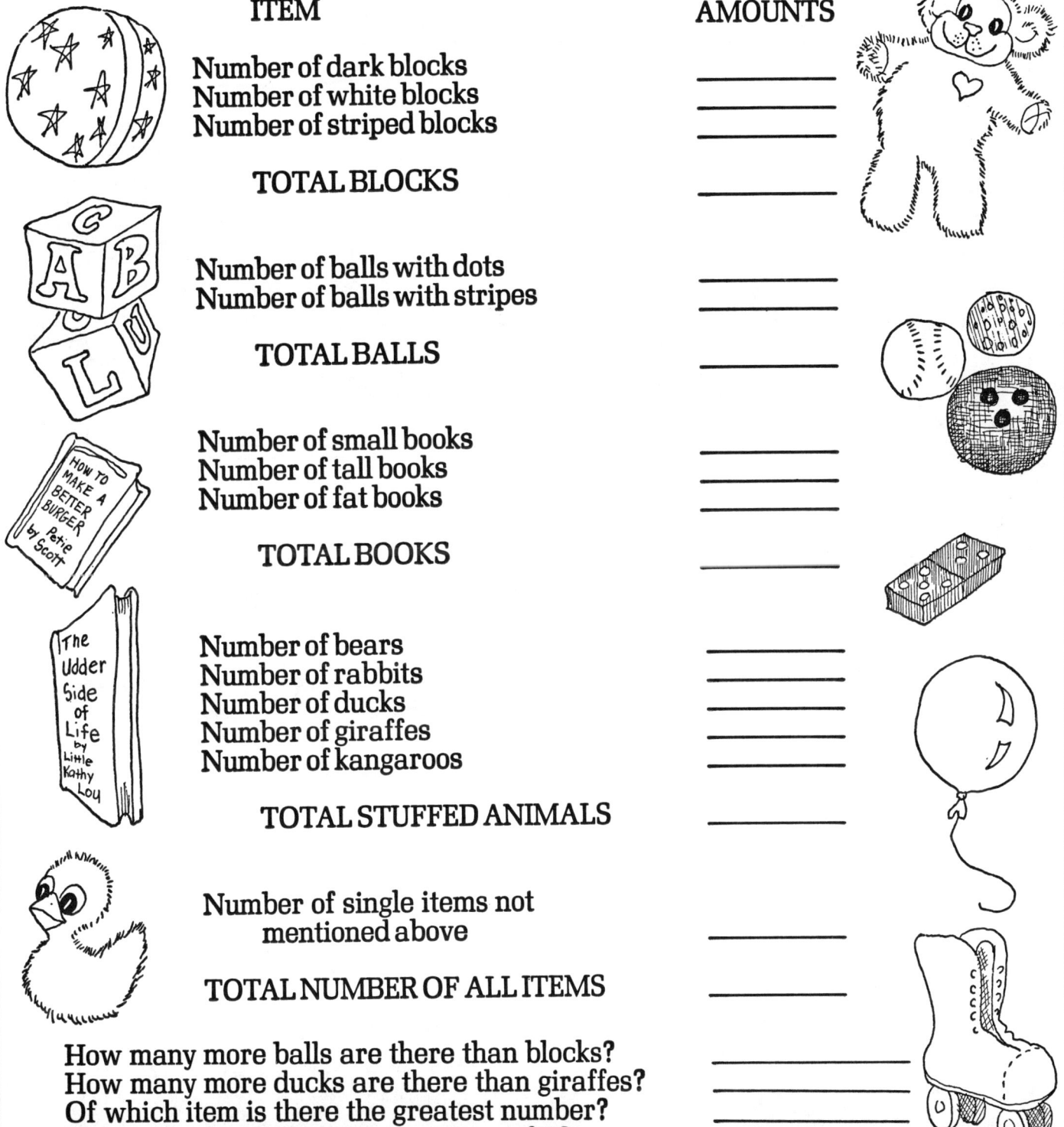

ITEM	AMOUNTS
Number of dark blocks	_____
Number of white blocks	_____
Number of striped blocks	_____
TOTAL BLOCKS	_____
Number of balls with dots	_____
Number of balls with stripes	_____
TOTAL BALLS	_____
Number of small books	_____
Number of tall books	_____
Number of fat books	_____
TOTAL BOOKS	_____
Number of bears	_____
Number of rabbits	_____
Number of ducks	_____
Number of giraffes	_____
Number of kangaroos	_____
TOTAL STUFFED ANIMALS	_____
Number of single items not mentioned above	_____
TOTAL NUMBER OF ALL ITEMS	_____

How many more balls are there than blocks? _____
How many more ducks are there than giraffes? _____
Of which item is there the greatest number? _____
How many items show an inventory of 3? _____

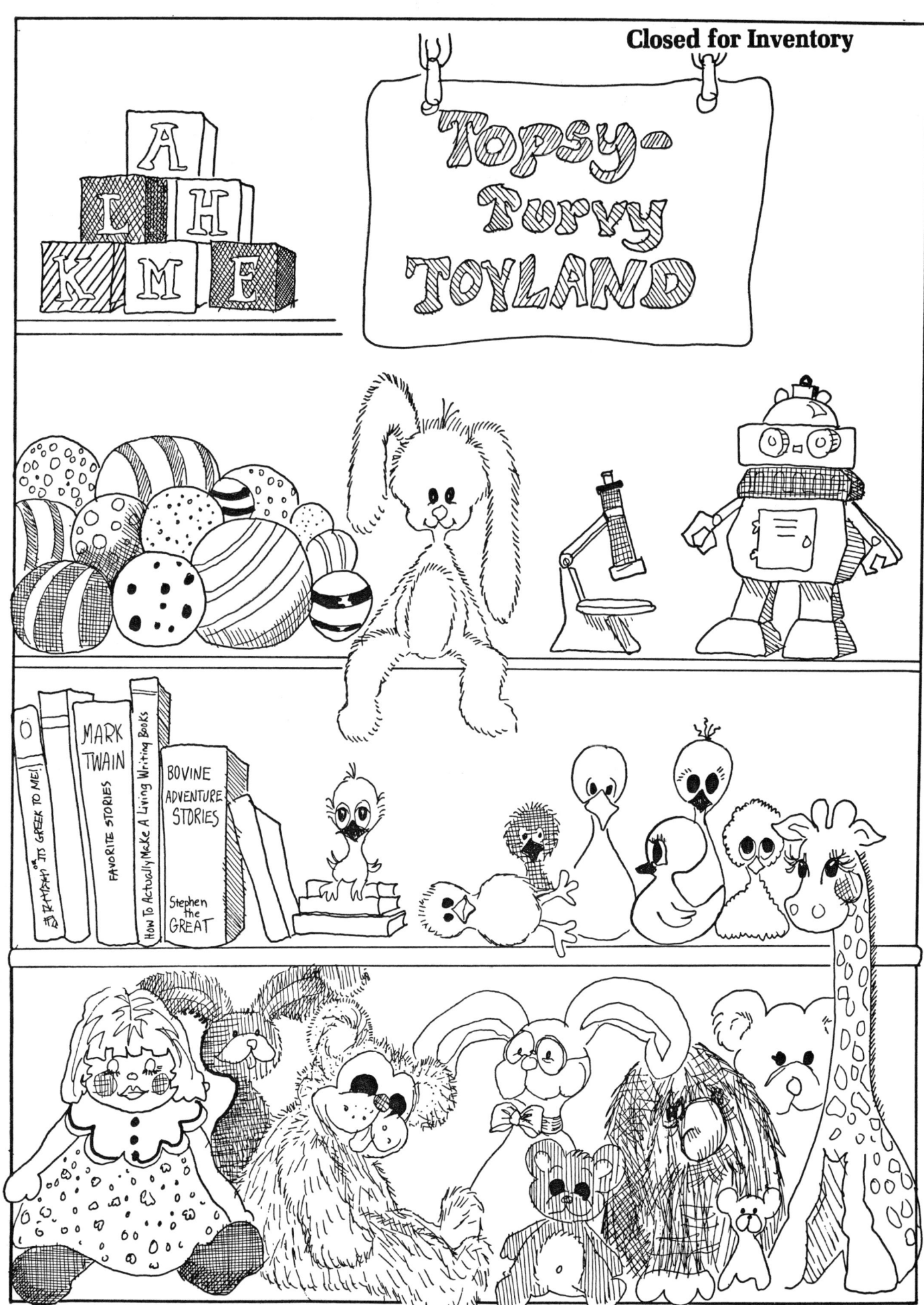

MYSTERY MANSION

Follow these directions to complete this activity.

1. Cut on the heavy black lines.
2. Fold on the dotted lines.
3. Line up pages 1 and 2 exactly and paste together at edges.
4. Open the windows and door. Solve the problems you find there.
5. After you have answered all the questions, figure out the solution to the Mystery Problem below. Write your answer in the space provided.

Mystery Problem: What does every problem in the Mystery Mansion have in common with every other problem?

Answer: _____

$20 + 7 - 3 + 10 =$ _____

John weighs 97 pounds. Mary weighs 85 lbs. How much more does John weigh than Mary? _____

```
   88
  172
  244
   18
 +267
 ____
```

```
  739
 -283
 ____
```

```
   4
   3
   5
   9
  +2
 ___
```

Jim has a marble collection of 312 marbles. He wants to divide them evenly with his 3 friends so that all 4 of them have an equal number of marbles. How many marbles will each have? _____

Joe has 74 baseball cards. Jill has 55. Bob has 69, and Joy has 70. What is the average number of baseball cards owned by members of this group? _____

WHICH IS WHICH?

Look at each pair of words in the center column. Decide which of those words is related to the word in the first column, and draw an arrow to it. Draw an arrow from the other word to the word related to it in the third column.

I	II	II
victory	one won	numeral
music	phrase frays	fight
humor	rye wry	bread
baker	dough doe	deer
war	guerillas gorillas	zoo
head	hare hair	rabbit
breakfast	serial cereal	TV
trees	suede swayed	shoes
baby	tiers tears	cake
wrestler	muscles mussels	ocean
destructive	bomb balm	soothing
game	pharaoh faro	Egypt
muscles	flex flecks	spots

105

A FAMILY PROBLEM

PURPOSE: Problem solving

PREPARATION: None

PROCEDURE
1. Present "A Family Problem" to the group, and lead a discussion of approaches to solving the problem.

2. The most obvious answers will probably be: 1) labeling the food with the name and date, and 2) arranging the food on the shelf in alphabetical order and always putting freshly frozen food on the back shelf so that the previously frozen food will be used first. Guide the discussion to continue until all possible solutions have been presented and tested.

Andrew's mother has a large vegetable garden. She freezes lots and lots of food from it for the family to eat during the winter months. Andrew and his three brothers and four sisters help with the gardening and freezing the foods. They use plastic freezer containers that their mother buys on sale at the corner market, and they save peanut butter and pickle jars to re-use. One big problem they have is knowing what is in what container, and which food has been frozen the longest and should be used first.

They freeze string beans, sweet corn, broccoli, red and green peppers, carrots, lima beans, cucumbers, peas, asparagus, and zucchini. Andrew thought of one way to solve this problem and his sister Amanda thought of another way. Can you think of these two ways and one more?

IT'S ALL CLASS!

The objects below can be classified in many different ways. For instance, all round objects could be grouped together, while all objects with straight edges could make up another group. The same objects could be reclassified according to which are usually used out-of-doors and which are usually used indoors. Other groups could be formed of those that are dark in color and those that are light in color.

Look at all the objects carefully, and complete the models on the following page. Then, make as many new classification groups as possible. (Use the back of your page if you need more room.)

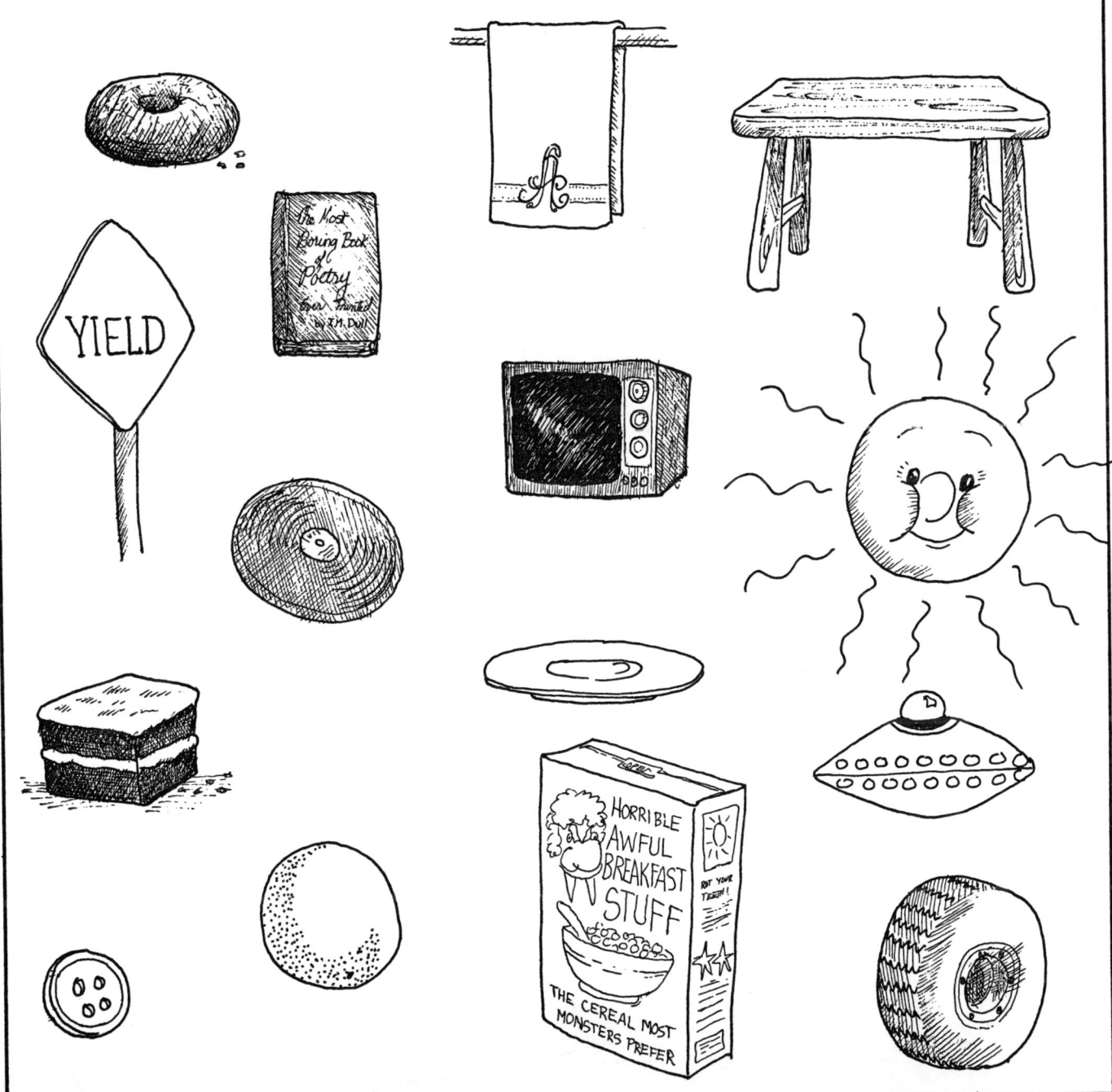

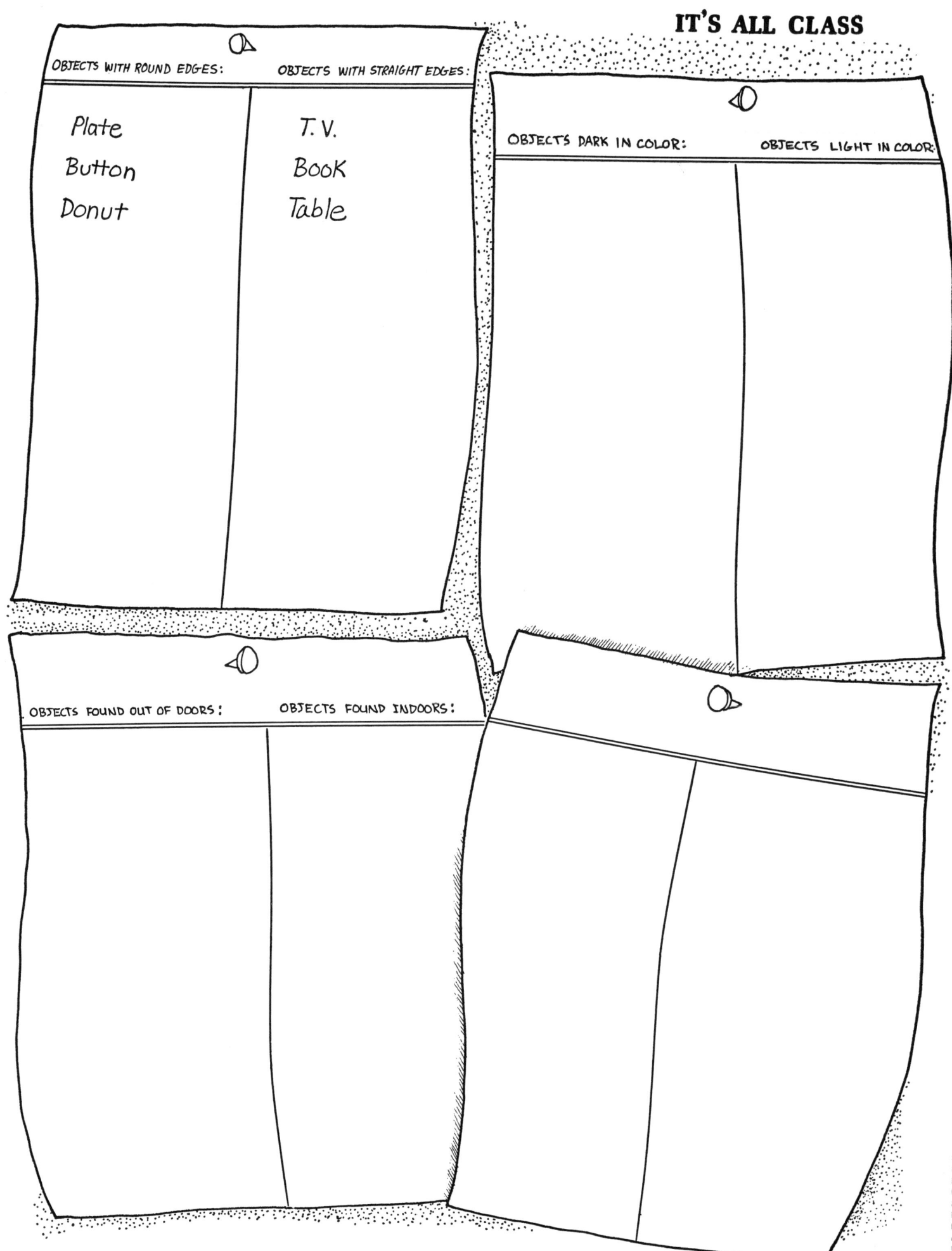

LOGICAL LINKS

Each problem on this page is a chain event! Figure out the final link in each chain, and write your answer in the empty link. Then, give your explanation of the logical progression pattern used in each problem in the space below it.

PATTERN: _____

PATTERN: _____

PATTERN: _____

PATTERN: _____

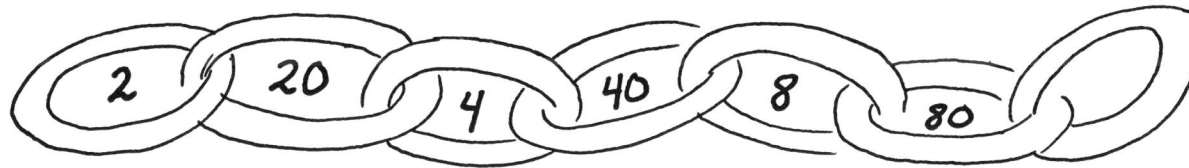

PATTERN: _____

PATTERN: _____

BODY LANGUAGE

There are many words associated with the human body that are also associated with other things. For instance, a bed has both a head and a foot, a river has a mouth, and another name for a computer is a brain.

Here is a labeled picture of the human body. Beside each label, write the names of other things that are also associated with that word.

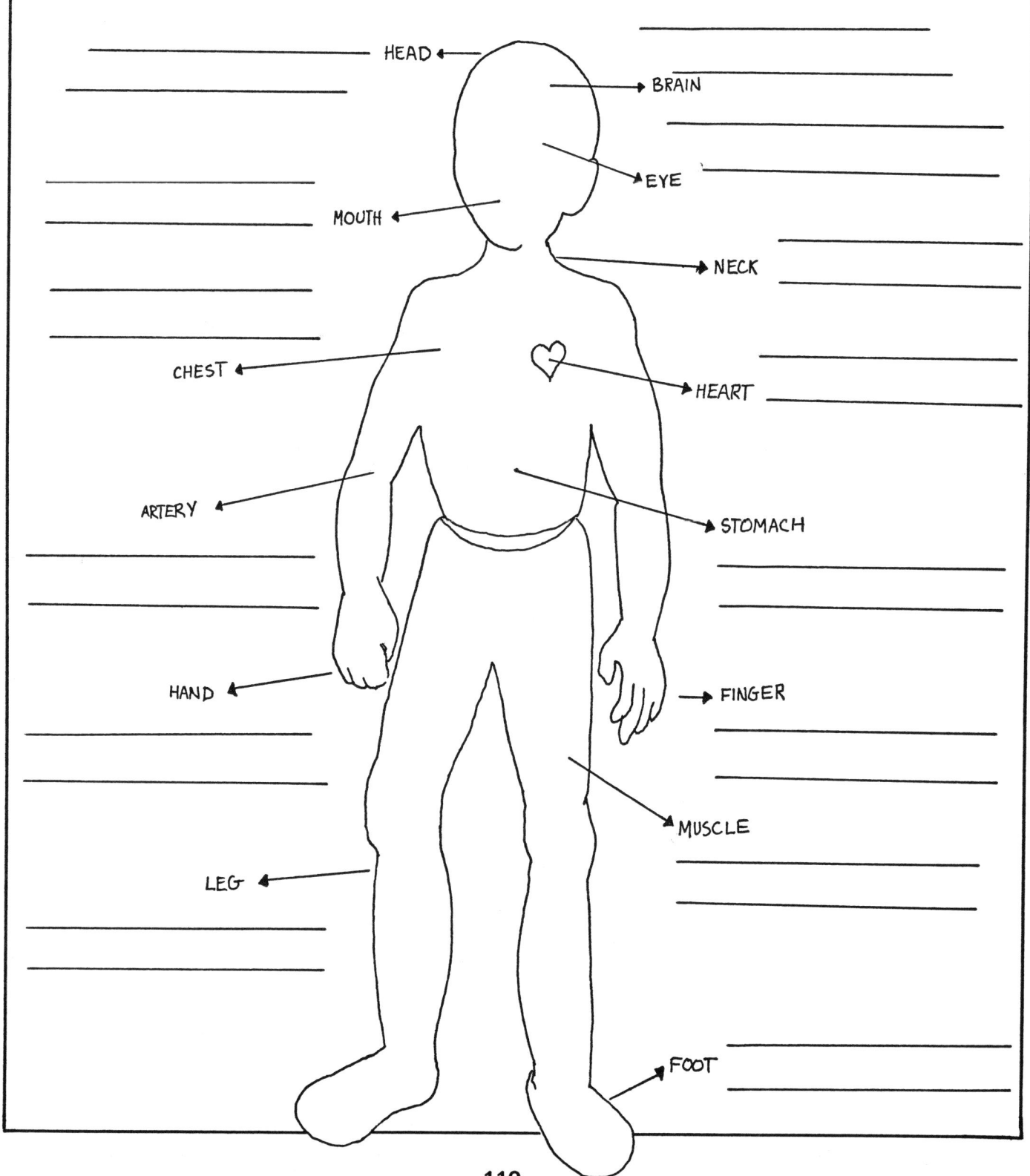

 # EXIT-OUT

Draw an X over the one word in each group that does not belong.

1. beef	veal	fish	pork	lamb
2. frolic	gambol	frisk	chance	romp
3. Tennessee	Michigan	Maine	Idaho	Florida
4. cardinal	henna	vermillion	red	crimson
5. badminton	tennis	racquetball	ping pong	volleyball
6. Georgia	Texas	Alabama	Arizona	Iowa
7. hideous	gruesome	repulsive	countenance	homely
8. Ford	Toyota	Dodge	Cadillac	Mercury
9. amateur	judge	connoisseur	epicure	critic
10. invertebrate	tipsy	bibulous	inebriate	intemperate
11. broom	perfume	tomb	brougham	pendulum
12. host	tenant	meteor	trustee	proprietor
13. epigraphy	stenography	calligraphy	paleography	topography
14. divorce	cohere	dissect	sever	separate
15. confident	summation	recognition	provider	terrify
16. amazon	venison	accordion	unison	vision
17. preserve	collect	acquire	obtain	procure
18. submissive	ambitious	approach	irrelevant	addition
19. alimony	subsidy	compensatory	stipend	bounty
20. Tom	Bob	John	Sue	Ann

111

WHO'S IN THE HAT?

All kinds of people wear hats! Some are very careful, neat, sophisticated characters. Others are the casual, carefree type.

Here are lots of hats. Point to the ones you think would fit with a sophisticated person. Then, touch all those a carefree person might wear. Compare the two groups. How are they alike? How are they different?

Choose two hats from each group and trace them on the activity page. For each, draw a head and body that goes with that type of hat. Draw a line underneath each picture, and write a name you've thought up for that person. Make the name match the hat and its personality.

Who's in the Hat?

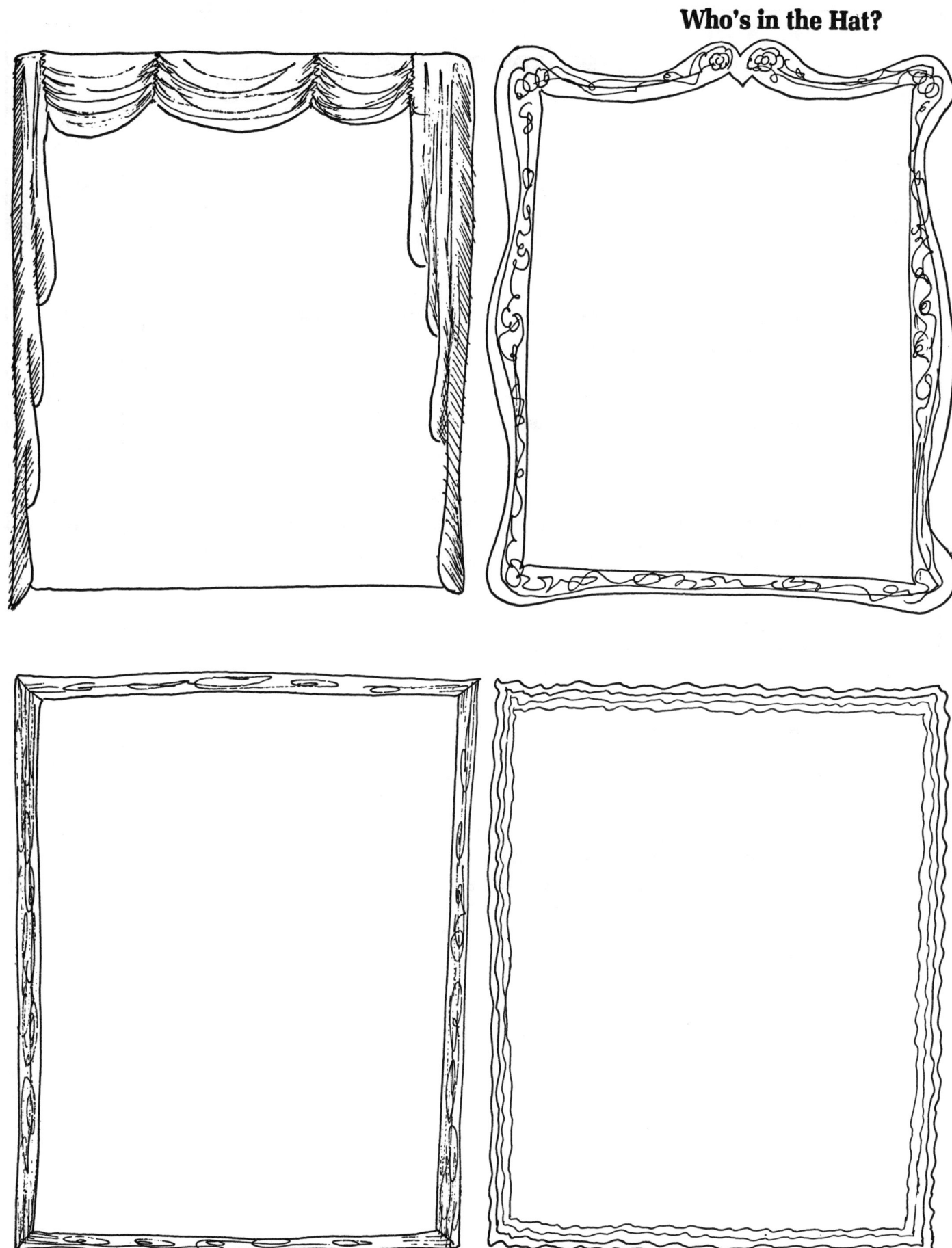

SPEAKING OF SURVEYS

PURPOSE: Surveying

PREPARATION
1. Write the word "survey" on the chalkboard.

2. In a brainstorming session, ask students to contribute their interpretations of the word and to name the kinds of surveys that come to mind immediately. List all suggestions on the board.

3. Continue the session by discussing ways surveys are made, who makes them, ways in which findings are organized and presented, and who profits from the results of various surveys. Keep the discussion going until all students have had a chance to express ideas.

4. Lead into an individual assignment with a realistic time limit, and give the students the following directions.

PROCEDURE
1. Select one of the following topics.

    (1) communicable diseases students in the class have had
    (2) the least favorite food served in the school cafeteria
    (3) changes taking place in the neighborhood or school
    (4) the favorite period of the school day
    (5) the number of out-of-school hours spent outside by members of the class
    (6) the number of library books read per week by members of the class
    (7) the popularity of various television programs
    (8) junk food eaten by members of the class

2. Develop a plan for conducting your survey. Put your plan into action, organize the results, and report your findings to the class.

114

TWO SIDES OF ME

PURPOSE: Abstracting

PREPARATION
1. Provide tempera paints, colored chalk or a wide selection of crayons, and a large sheet (at least 18" x 24") of tag or heavy construction paper for each student.

PROCEDURE
1. Ask students to consider their personal qualities or attributes, both positive and negative.

2. Work together as a class to list as many of these as possible on the chalkboard.

3. Then, ask each student to choose one positive quality and one negative quality which are especially characteristic of his/her own personality.

4. Direct students to select one or more colors that represent or express the essences of their positive qualities, and use these colors to create a design that suggests that quality. (This design should cover one side of the paper.)

   Example: joyful; exuberant

   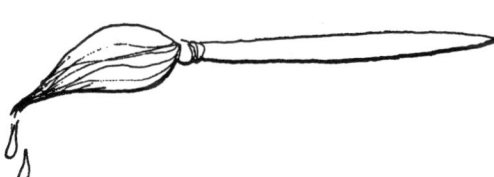

5. Repeat the same process for the negative quality. (This design should fill the entire surface of the other side of the paper.)

   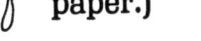

   Example: fearful

   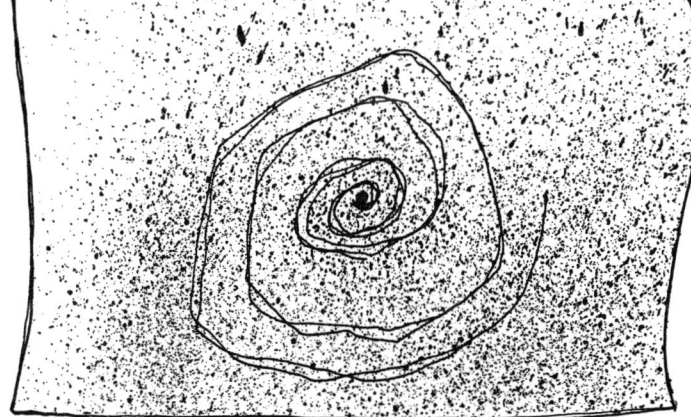

6. Students may share their designs and ask classmates to guess the qualities illustrated.

115

Who Has The BUTTON?

Here are pictures of 5 characters. Behind each character, there is an object which you cannot see.

The 5 objects are:
    an arrow   a button   a bone   a star   a mop

However, they are not in this order.

Given the information below, see if you can figure out which character has the BUTTON!

1. The BONE is not next to the MOP, and neither is the STAR.
2. The STAR is not next to the BUTTON, and neither is the BONE.
3. The MOP is not next to the ARROW, and neither is the STAR.
4. The BUTTON is just to the left of the ARROW.

_____ has the BUTTON!!

A BIG BAG BUY

This bag is manufactured by the Super Bag Company, 218 West Main Street, Chicago, Illinois 60601. It looks and feels like leather, but it is really made of top quality vinyl that can be wiped clean with a damp cloth.

It comes in brown, navy blue, or bone, and has an adjustable shoulder strap and a gold-look metal clasp. The bag is lined with good quality rayon fabric. Additional inside features include a removable change purse, a mirror, an address book, and a memo pad.

Create a newspaper ad to sell the bag.

A Big Bag Buy

Design a one-page mail order advertisement to sell the bag. Redraw it, and show all the additional pieces.

Use this checklist to be sure the bag has been advertised in the best way possible to make every person on the mail order list a buyer.

____ Descriptive words used
____ Heavy, bold lettering used in titles
____ All uses stressed
____ Graphics clear and concise
____ Price and shipping charges clearly stated
____ Reliability of company stated
____ All information included on order blank

QUOTABLE QUOTES

The letters you see in the columns below the puzzle fit into the boxes directly above them, but not necessarily in the order listed. Decide which letter goes into which box and write it in. As you use each letter, cross it off. When you are finished, you will have a famous quotation by Thomas Alva Edison.

C	C	E	N	T	P	E	T	S	P	N	R	A	T	I	P	P	R	A
N	E	G	N	N	I	I	N	Y	I	I	I	N	E	E	O	E	E	R
	D	N	E	I	N	E	R	S	P	S	R	O	N	I	O	N		
			T			U	S			I		A	T			N		

Choose a different famous quotation and use the empty grid below to create a similar puzzle of your own.

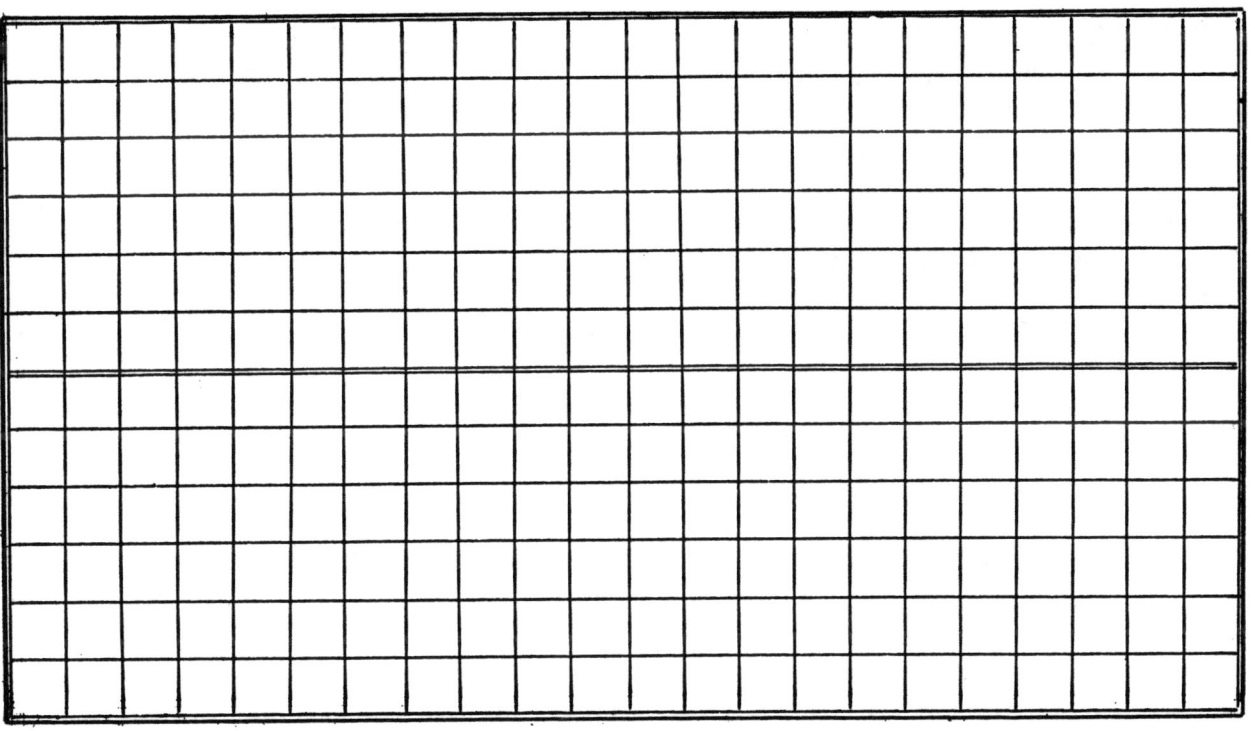

119

TALE OF TWO CITIES

PURPOSE: Generalizing

PREPARATION
1. Duplicate one set of the following activity pages for each student.

2. Provide crayons, pencils, and paper.

PROCEDURE
1. Direct students to study the pictures of Valleyville and Progressport.

2. Ask students to make a list on the back of each picture of as many words as possible that could be used to describe that city in general. Allow 20 minutes for this activity; then, share and compare the generalizations about the two cities.

3. Now, ask students to color both pictures. When they have finished, direct them to write three statements on the back of each page that make additional generalizations about that city. Allow 30 minutes for this activity; then, allow students to share their ideas. (These generalizations should differ somewhat because of the choices of colors used.)

4. Compare and contrast answers, and discuss possible reasons for choices and differences.

Tale of Two Cities

121

Tale of Two Cities

ANALYSIS COMPETENCY REVIEW

Use the picture-poster above to help you answer the questions. Circle the correct answer (or answers) to each question.

1. Which class contains four of the above characters?

    those wearing hats
    those with bald heads
    those holding an object or wearing some equipment
    those who are taller than the referee

2. Which item below tells how many of the characters have their legs completely covered?

    exactly half of them
    less than half of them
    more than half of them
    none of them

3. Which statements are true?
    The baby is wearing more clothes than the tallest man.
    The lady in high heels has the largest hat.
    The space creature and the scuba diver are taller than the boy.

4. What is the number of characters not wearing shoes?

    four   three
    six   none

5. Which description accurately tells how this group could be separated?

    a group of two and a group of three
    two groups of four
    a group of five and a group of two
    three groups of two

6. Which would be a solution for this problem?

    All seven characters must go to town in a bus with only 4 seats.

    Someone could hold the baby.
    Everyone but the driver would share a seat.
    The scuba diver should leave all equipment at home.

7. If you removed the headwear from all the characters, which of these would be the shortest?

   the lady in the polka dot dress
   the boy with the airplane
   the scuba diver
   the space creature

8. The whistle is to the referee as:

   the diaper pin is to the baby.
   the snorkel is to the scuba diver.
   the flippers are to the scuba diver.
   the ears are to the space creature.

9. In which pair are the items most unlike each other?

   the tall man's legs and the baby's legs
   the lady's dress and the boy's shirt
   the tall man's shorts and the referee's shirt
   the scuba diver's flippers and the space creature's feet

10. The question that would best help you determine the hobbies of the characters would be:

    "Why do you have on that outfit?"
    "How much free time do you have?"
    "Do you like sports?"
    "What do you do for fun and relaxation?"

11. Which of the following can you assume to be true?

    The lady should go on a diet.
    The boy ate spaghetti for lunch.
    The baby's diaper is wet.
    The space creature is dangerous.

12. Which phrase best advertises the poster pictures on the first page?

    "A poster you'll definitely want!"
    "A smashing, humorous poster of seven unique characters."
    "A line-up of interesting people."
    "See seven separate personalities."

13. If there were a hidden code in this picture related to the letters in the characters' names, which of these could be the secret word?

    octopus   peacock
    quacking   barnacle

14. Which statements would you choose as accurate?

    Most of the characters are wearing something on their heads.
    Everyone's feet are dirty.
    The females are all wearing dresses.
    Very few of the characters have on watches.

SKILLSTUFF

SYNTHESIS

IV. SYNTHESIS SKILLS AND PROCESSES — SKILLSTUFF Activities

- ____ Inferring
- ____ Extending
- ____ Imagining
- ____ Hypothesizing
- ____ Rearranging
- ____ Magnifying
- ____ Formulating
- ____ Visualizing
- ____ Reversing
- ____ Combining
- ____ Summarizing
- ____ Creating
- ____ Designing
- ____ Encoding
- ____ Producing
- ____ Modifying
- ____ Refining
- ____ Minimizing
- ____ Inventing
- ____ Substituting
- ____ Maximizing
- ____ Composing
- ____ Conceptualizing
- ____ Proposing
- ____ Organizing

TO THE RESCUE

Fill in each blank with the correct word from the list at the bottom of the page to find out what is happening here.

"R_____!" squealed the r_____. "R_____ to my r_____! The r_____ old r_____ will r_____ over my r_____, r_____ r_____ and r_____ them forever!"

ruin   run   rescue   ride
rabbit   radishes   robot   rush
red   rusty   rosy

TO BUILD A BOAT

1. Begin with one letter.

2. Add another letter to that to make a two-letter word.

3. Add a third letter to make a three-letter word.

4. Add a fourth letter to make a four-letter word.

Add letters to build these boats.

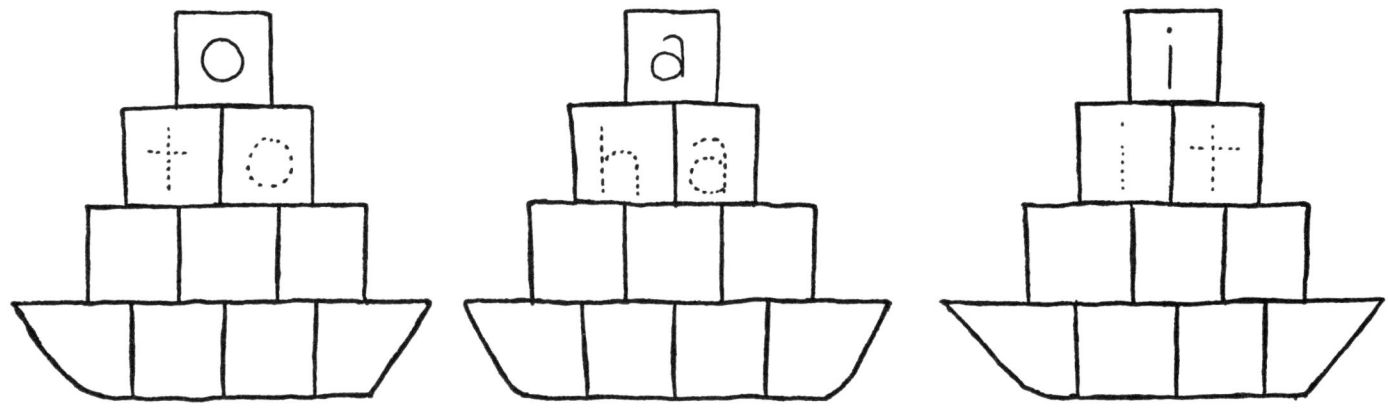

Build some more boats that are all your own.

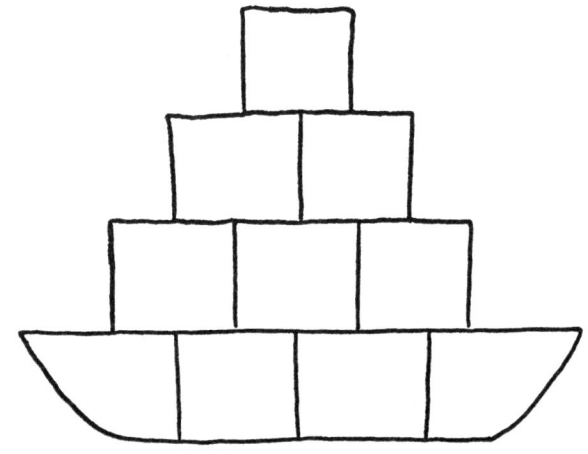

LAND OF THE GIANTS

PURPOSE: Imagining

PREPARATION
1. Cut out a pair of huge paper boots for each person in the class. Help students attach these to the front legs of their chairs.

2. Ask each student to bring from home an adult-sized long coat, a pair of old gloves, and a hat.

PROCEDURE
1. Help students stuff gloves and pin them to the coat sleeves.

2. Arrange "booted" chairs in a line or large circle.

3. Make each child a giant by helping him don the large coat and hat, and stand on the chair with the coat hanging down over the paper boots.

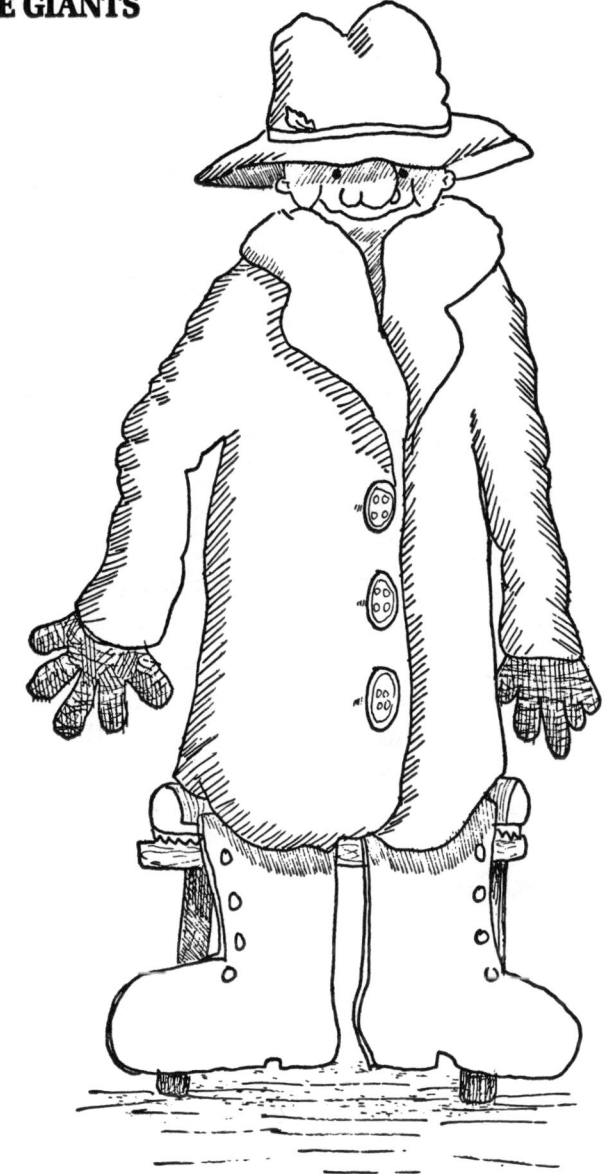

4. Invite a kindergarten or first grade class to visit your "Land of the Giants."

5. Appoint several "giants" to act as interviewers to ask the visitors how it feels to be a very short person in a land of very tall people.

6. When the fun is over, engage students in a language experience in which all contribute to a story about a very small person who visits the "Land of the Giants." The story should focus upon how this person feels.

WHAT IS IT?

PURPOSE: Hypothesizing

PREPARATION
1. Divide students into three groups.

2. Make a copy of the first activity page for each member of group #1, a copy of the second activity page for each member of group #2, and a copy of the third activity page for each member of group #3.

3. Prepare for each student a cover page of dark construction paper in which holes have been randomly punched. Staple one over each activity sheet. Secure at top, bottom, and sides so the student cannot see the activity page except through the holes in the cover sheet.

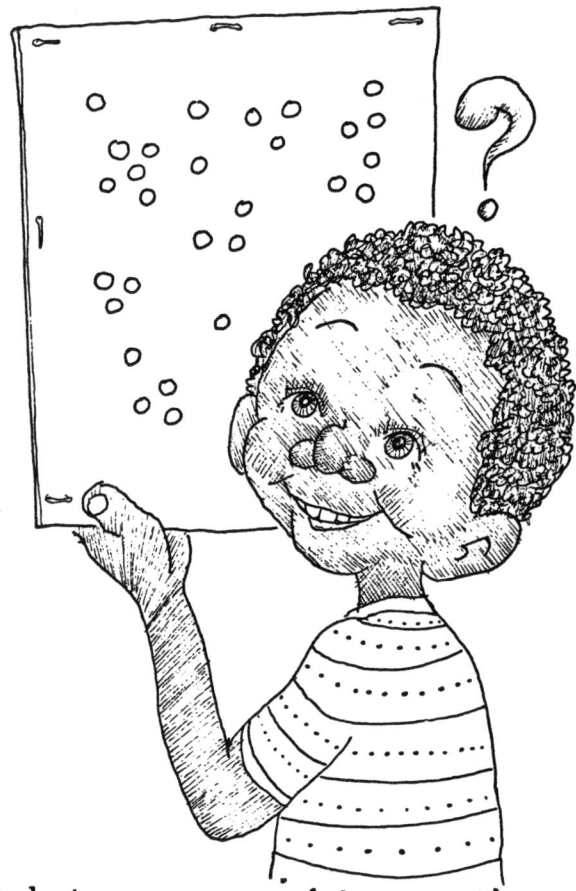

PROCEDURE
1. Distribute the covered activity pages to the students.

2. Explain to the students that an object is pictured on the covered page. Their task is to hypothesize as to what that object might be by looking through the punched holes.

3. Direct students to consider each hole separately, look at each carefully, decide what the object might be if it appears as it looks through that single opening, and write down that decision beside the hole.

4. After students have considered each hole and made their guesses, they review these and make a general hypothesis of what the entire picture is.

5. Students return to their groups to share their hypotheses and combine their ideas to make one hypothesis. When this has been agreed upon, students may tear off the cover sheets to check their hypotheses (and color their pictures if desired).

   Note: These activity pages may be used as motivation for brainstorming, vocabulary extention, and/or springboards to creative writing.

130

What Is It?

What Is It?

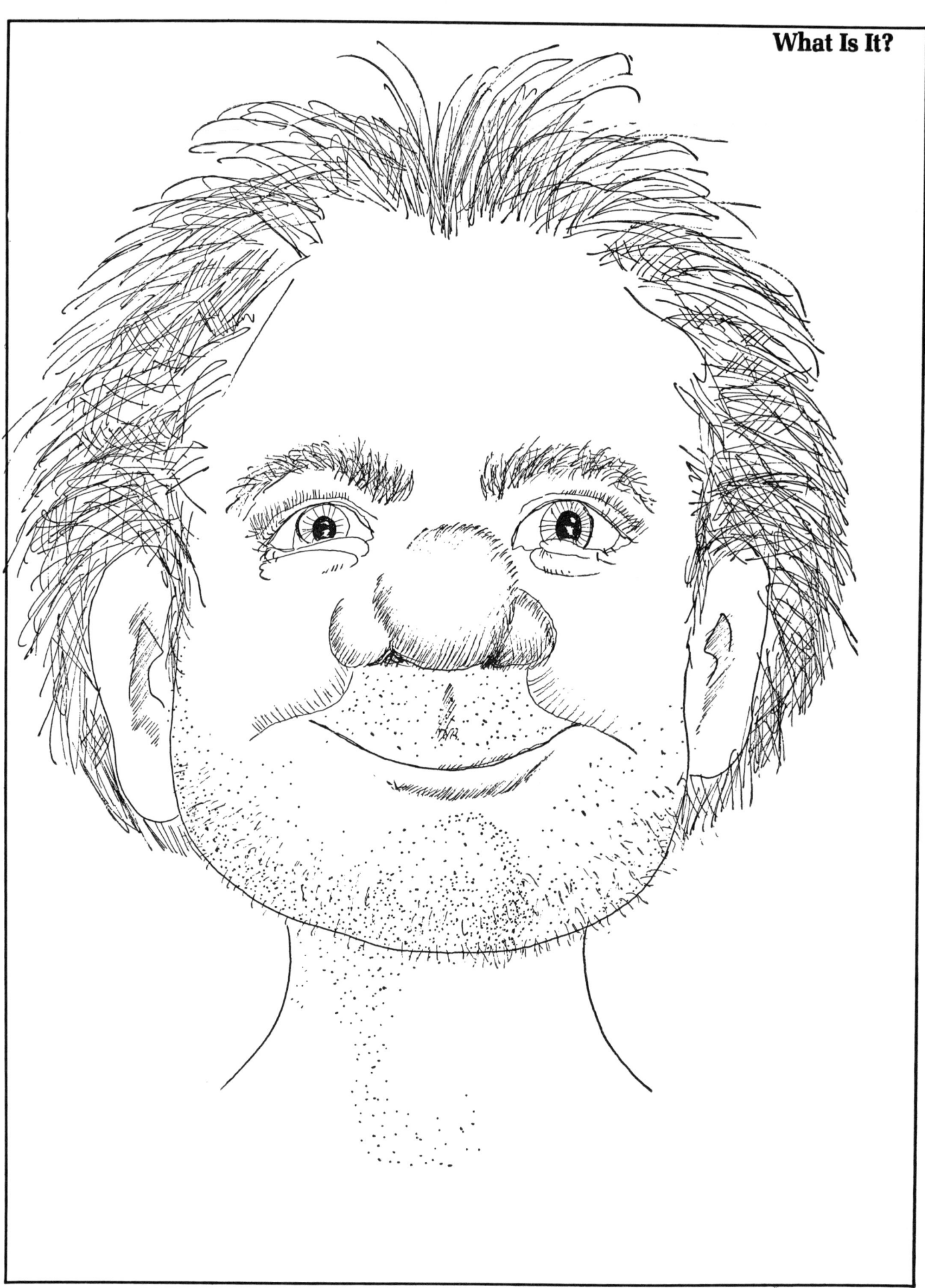

What Is It?

SENTENCE SENSE

Rearrange the words in these sentences to make two new sentences. Remember, a sentence always expresses a complete thought and must make sense.

1. The mail will arrive soon.
   _____.
   _____?

2. I can't believe you saw the snake first.
   _____.
   _____?

3. We did hear a noise behind the door.
   _____.
   _____?

4. We could go to the fair later.
   _____.
   _____?

Make two sentences on your own, and rewrite them to make two new sentences.

5. _____.
   _____.
   _____?

6. _____.
   _____.
   _____?

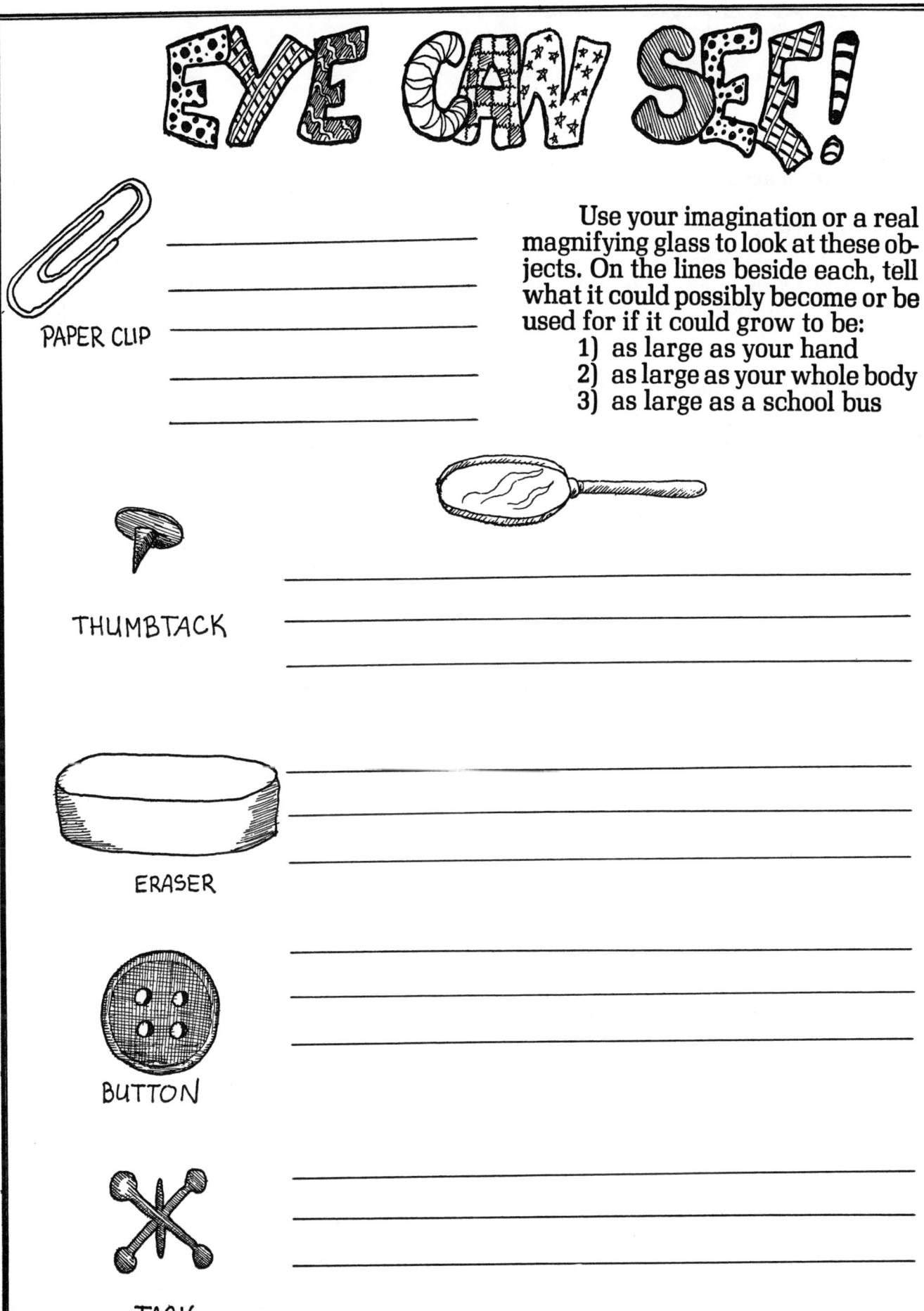

SPEAKING PERSONALLY

PURPOSE: Imagining

PREPARATION

1. Print phrases presenting a non-human character in a perplexing situation on strips of paper or tagboard. Use the phrases on the following pages and/or some of your own for "starters." (Students will enjoy adding their own to the collection, too.)

2. Cut the strips apart, and put each one in a separate envelope.

3. Print "Speaking Personally" on the cover of a notebook to hold completed stories.

4. Place the envelopes, pencils, and writing paper with the notebook in a free choice interest center. Add a study guide on which the following directions have been printed.

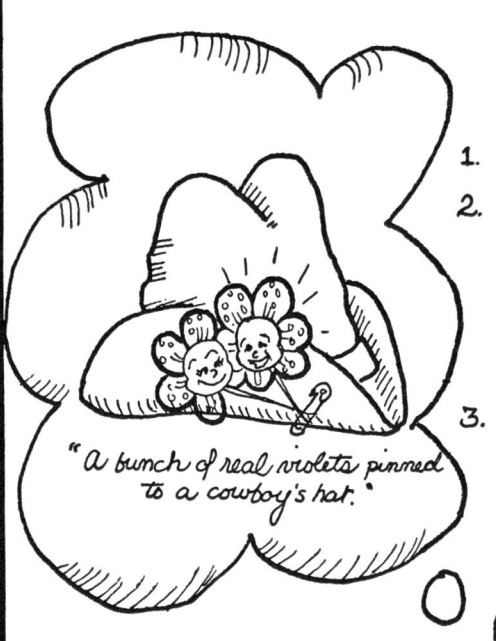

"a bunch of real violets pinned to a cowboy's hat."

Speaking Personally

1. Select one of the envelopes.
2. Use the story starter inside to write a first-person story. Imagine that you are the object, and use the situation given as the basis for your plot.
3. Illustrate your story, and add it to the "Speaking Personally" story book.

Speaking Personally

THE WORD MACHINE

Feed each of the following through the Word Machine (your brain) and come up with a brand new, not-yet-heard-of word for each.

a person who always puts his foot in his mouth _____

a meal made entirely of leftovers _____

a machine that would automatically give you a computerized print-out of all test answers for a given subject _____

an unexpected and totally unappreciated homework assignment _____

an instrument that could measure whether or not a person is in love _____

a day that was predicted by all forecasters to be sunny but turned out nasty _____

MEET THE GIP

Hello! I'd like to introduce you to my friend the Gip. Let me describe him to you.

He has a stout, rather heavy body which is covered with coarse, bristly hair. His head and short, thick neck extend in a straight line from his body, which is horizontal to the ground. The head ends in a snout, which is a broad, leathery pad that includes large nostrils. He uses this snout to dig. He has tiny eyes and very sharp teeth. His short tail is usually curled. My friend has four feet with four toes on each foot.

Now, draw a picture of my friend the Gip in the space below.

Keep your drawing a secret until you have finished. Then, compare it with the drawings done by your classmates. Does the Gip's picture remind you of an animal you have met before?

After you have shared your drawings, your teacher will show you a picture of my friend.

It's Reversible!

PURPOSE: Reversing

PREPARATION
1. Propose to the class that this coming Friday be a "Backwards Day." Ask them to help you plan a day during which everything that would normally take place on this day would be done in reverse.

2. Brainstorm for suggestions, and write the ideas given on the chalkboard.

> **BACKWARDS DAY!**
> - WEAR CLOTHES BACKWARDS.
> - COMPLETE DAILY SCHEDULE FROM END TO BEGINNING.
> - WALK BACKWARDS.
> - SPELL NAMES BACKWARDS ON NAME TAGS AND CALL PEOPLE BY THEIR "BACKWARDS" NAMES.
> - DO ALL MATH PROBLEMS BACKWARDS. (IF IT SAYS ADD, SUBTRACT; IF IT SAYS MULTIPLY, DIVIDE.)
> - GIVE DIRECTIONS IN OPPOSITES. (I.E. "DO NOT GO TO LUNCH" MEANS "GO TO LUNCH.")

3. When the brainstorming session is complete, use the collected ideas to plan the day together.

4. Have a happy, crazy, backwards Friday!!

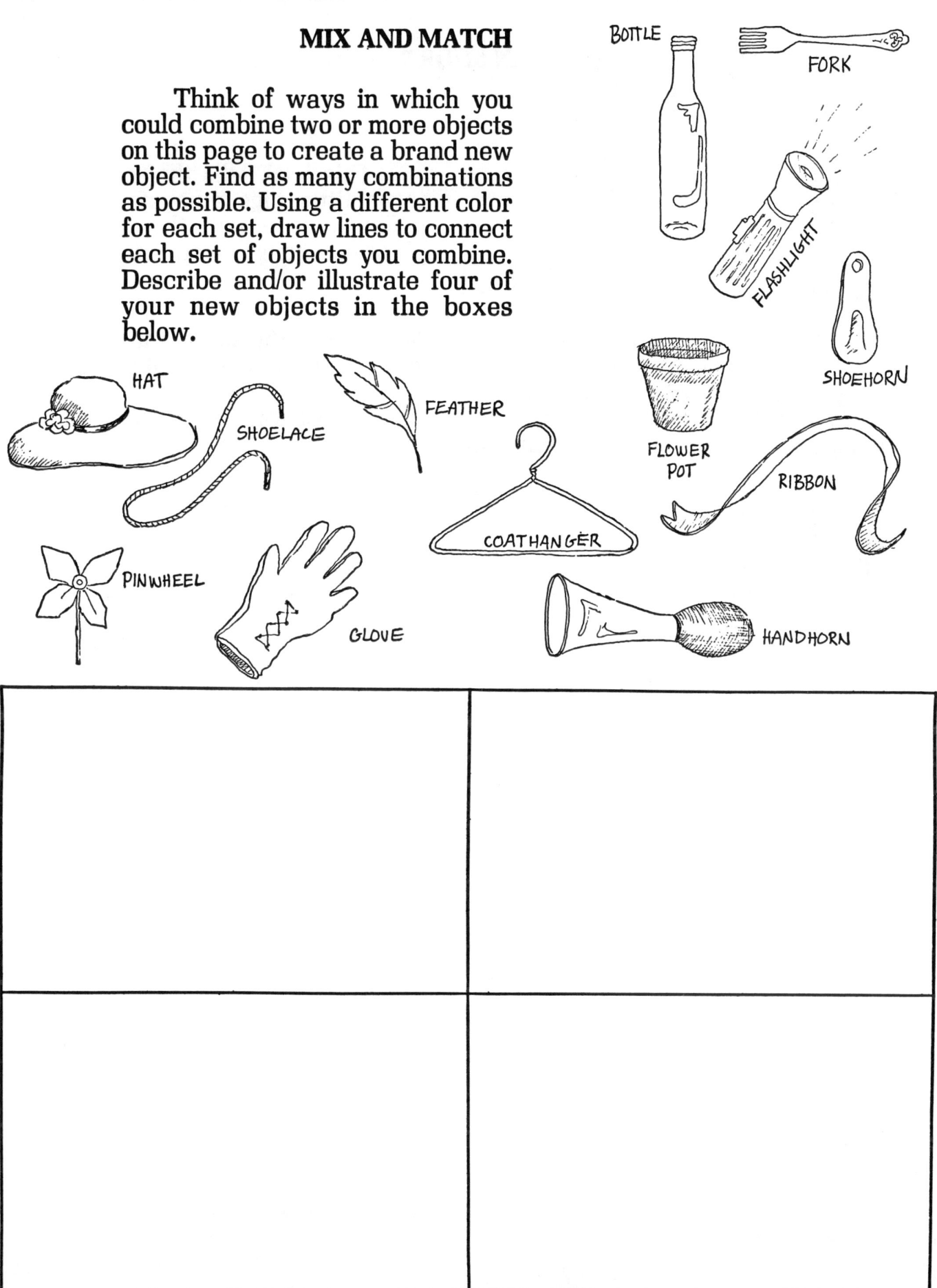

IN SHORT

This book tells the story of three little pigs who struggled valiantly to outwit the vicious plans of a hungry wolf, and won!

The paragraph you see above is a SUMMARY of the story of the "Three Little Pigs." A summary is a very brief retelling of the most important points of a story or any body of information.

Below there are three story titles which you probably know well. Write a summary of each story on the lines provided.

Cinderella

_____
_____
_____
_____
_____
_____

Pinocchio

_____
_____
_____
_____
_____
_____

The Tortoise and the Hare

_____
_____
_____
_____
_____

JUNGLE JOURNEY

As you take your Jungle Journey, follow the instructions on each page.

Pebble Beach

Your first stop is Pebble Beach. Use the letters on the pebbles to make as many words of more than two letters as possible. (You may use a pebble more than once in a word.) Write your words in the sand.

Jungle Journey

VALLEY OF THE LITTLE PEOPLE

You are now entering the Valley of the Little People. Unscramble each set of letters to find the names of all the kinds of people who live here.

FWARDS _____

SNRIBWOE _____

SPIIEX _____

ONGMES _____

MELSRING _____

SCHAUNPREEL _____

HPSNMY _____

RAIIFES _____

LEVES _____

SMIP _____

144

Jungle Journey

CRITTER CROSSING

This is Critter Crossing. Read the clues to identify the critters that come to this place.

1. 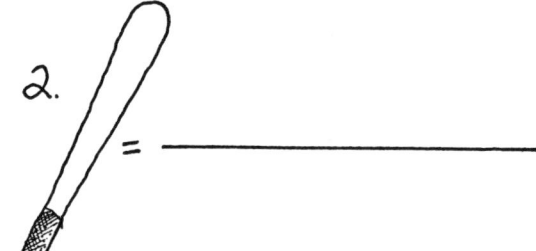 + L + SOAP − S = _____

2. 🏏 = _____

3. A ♥ = _____

4. 👩 + 🕷 = _____

5. F + 📦 − B = _____

6. 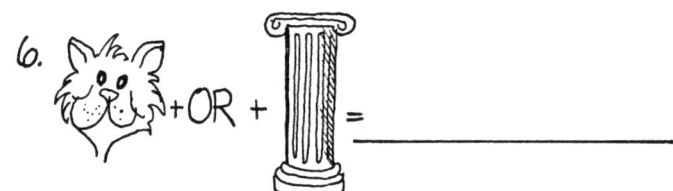 +OR + 🏛 = _____

7.  = _____

8. 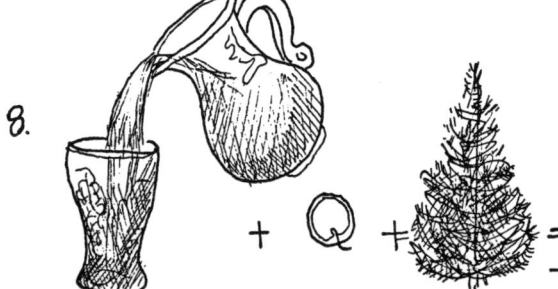 + Q + 🌲 = _____

Jungle Journey

FIELD OF FLOWERS

On each petal, write a word that goes with the word in the center of the flower.

147

IT'S YOUR GAME

PURPOSE: Creating

PREPARATION

1. Reproduce the two pages of the gameboard for each student.

2. Provide a manila file folder for each student, along with glue, sheets of unlined paper, pencils, crayons, felt pens, colored construction paper, scissors, index cards, and envelopes.

3. Discuss and list on the chalkboard the many uses and purposes of educational game boards.

4. Distribute the two halves of the blank gameboard and the file folders. Make sure the other supplies are accessible to students for free time use.

5. Provide the following instructions.

It's Your Game

PROCEDURE

1. Use the materials to design a game to teach or reinforce a specific skill.

2. Plan the entire game, including patterns, dice, tokens, game cards, etc., on scrap paper.

3. Arrange your gameboard sheets as you wish, and paste them into the folder.

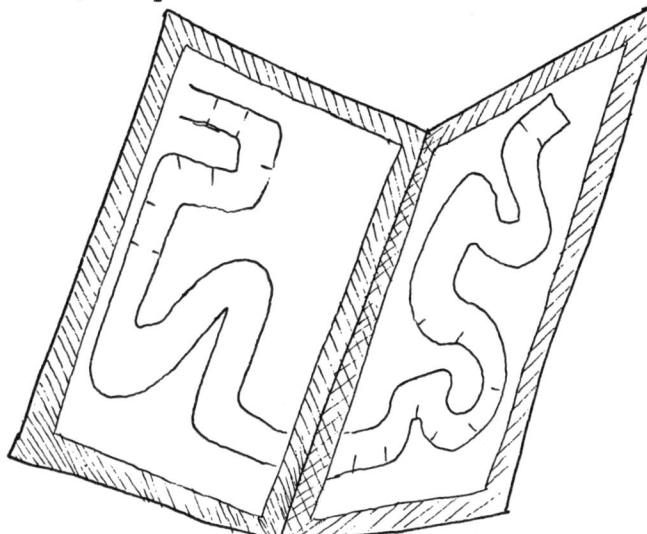

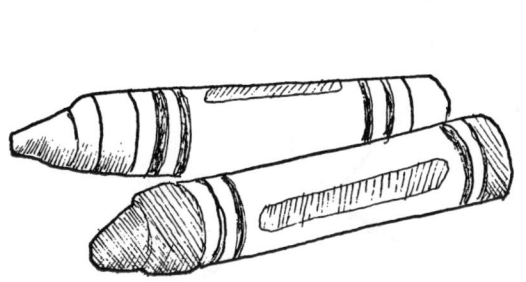

4. Complete the game board by adding directions and illustrations. Use crayons, felt pens, pencils, and/or construction paper cut-outs.

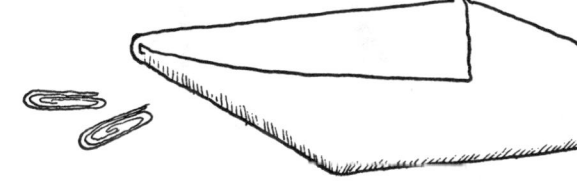

5. Make all supporting materials and place these in an envelope to be clipped inside the game folder.

6. Print the name of the game, the purpose, and rules for playing the game on the outside of the folder.

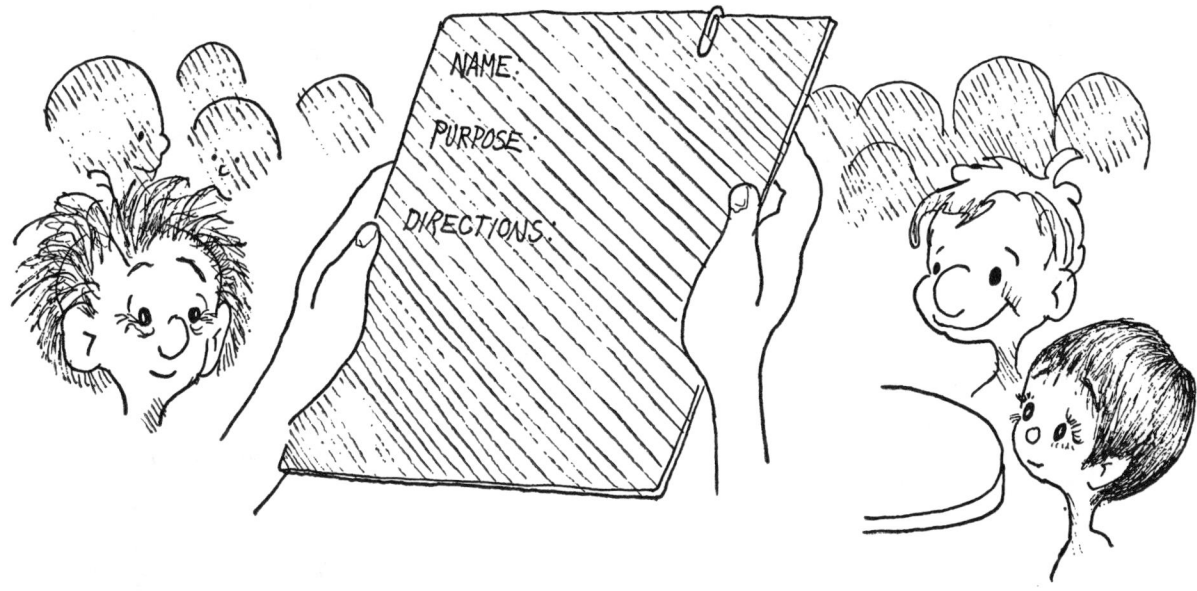

7. Place your game in the game center for your classmates to evaluate, enjoy, and learn from.

It's Your Game

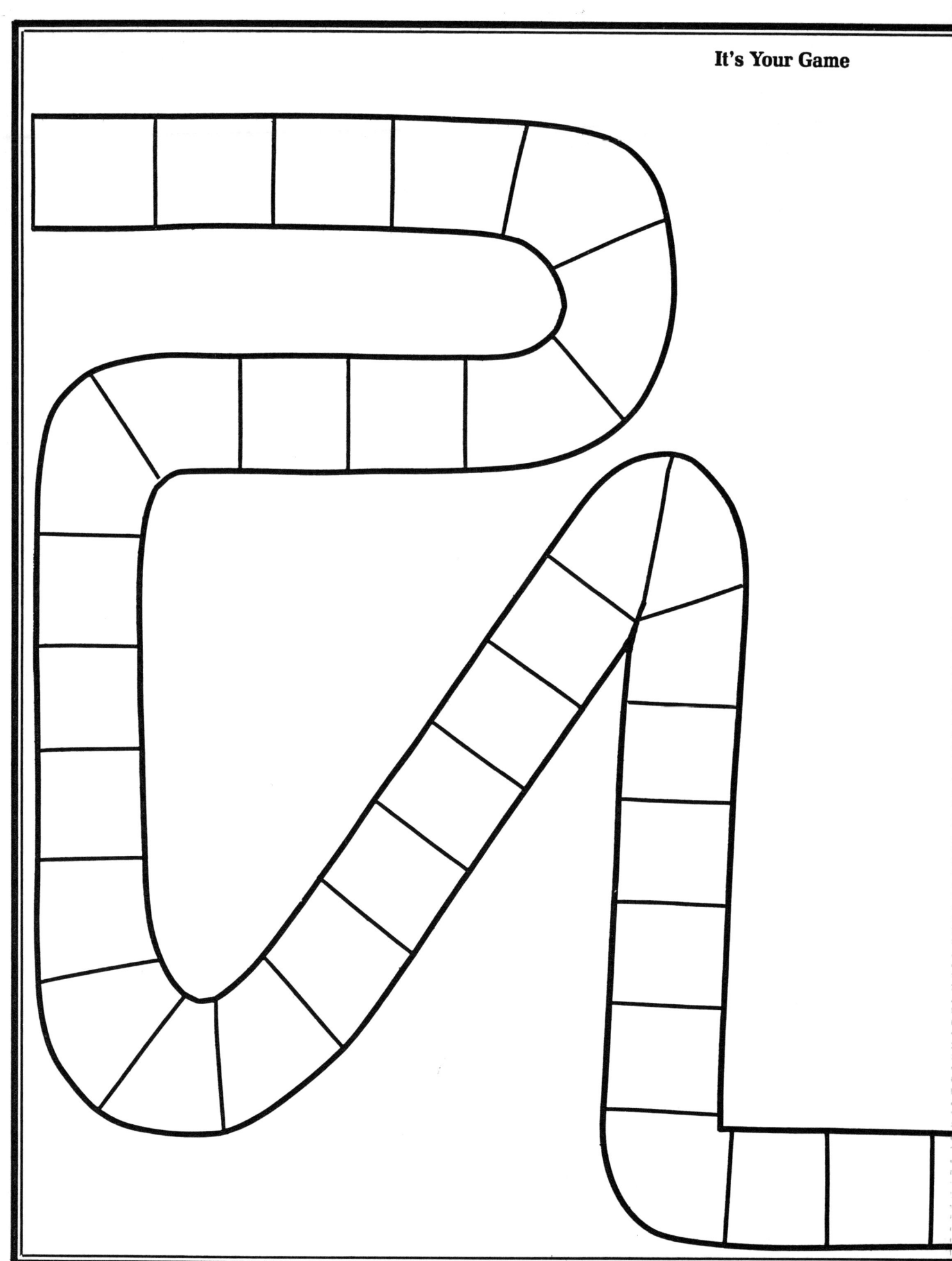

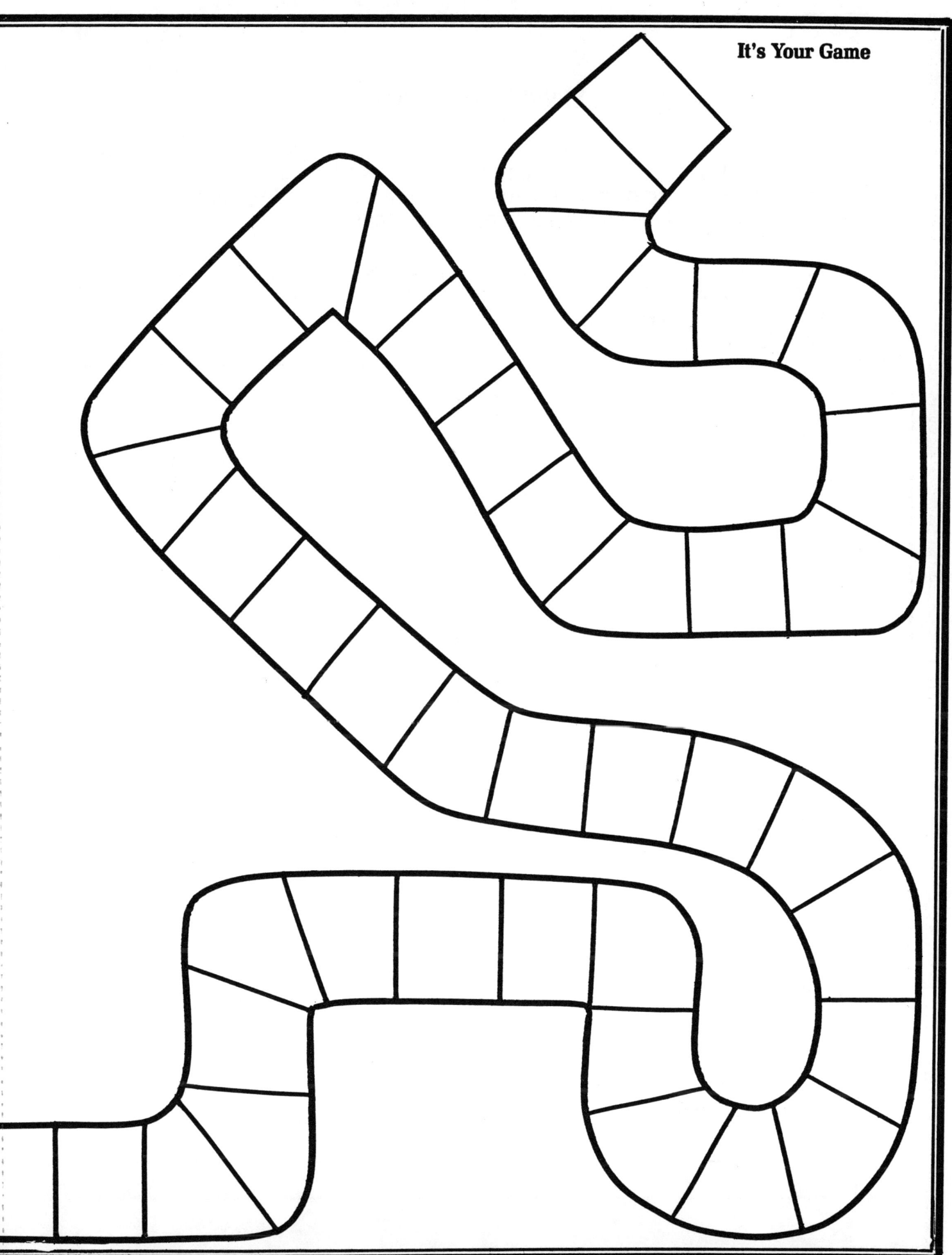

PERFECT PACKING

Look through catalogs for various types of traveling bags. Note the differences in styles, sizes, types of materials used, and prices.

Select a person to design the absolutely perfect traveling bag for...
  your neighbor, your best friend, your teacher,
    yourself, or someone else.

Think about that person's occupation, personal tastes, places the person is apt to go, methods of transportation the person might use, and the things he or she would need to take along.

Sketch the bag.

Outside Sketch   *Inside Sketch*

Give the following information:

Dimensions: _____

Materials: _____

Catalog Description: _____
_____

Price: $_____

CODED COMMUNICATION

Create a secret code that you have never used before. Cut out the three telegram forms on these two pages, and use them to send a coded message to three of your friends. Send the identical message to each, and write the name of the receiver in the code on the line provided on each telegram form. (This will give the receiver the hint needed to "crack" your code.)

Deliver the telegrams to all three friends at the same time, and see which one can decode the message first!

Coded Communication

CODED MESSAGE FOR: _____

　MESSAGE: _____

_____

_____

_____

_____

_____

_____

CODED MESSAGE FOR: _____

　MESSAGE: _____

_____

_____

_____

_____

_____

_____

Party Producer

PURPOSE: Producing and Proposing

PREPARATION
1. Write this list on the chalkboard.

Mozart	a pet rock
State of Texas	your oldest tennis shoe
Golden Gate Bridge	Mississippi River
an ant	Washington Monument
spring	the hit that made the winning run in the World Series
Peter Rabbit	
Sherlock Holmes	a mermaid
Declaration of Independence	Cleopatra
the moon	Johnny Appleseed
Father Time	the first automobile

2. Reproduce a copy of the "Party Producer" activity page for each student.

PROCEDURE
1. Tell students you are commissioning each of them to produce a huge birthday party to be given in honor of one of the "personalities" listed above. Each "producer" must plan his/her entire party using the accompanying activity page as a guide.

2. Divide students into small groups of 5 or 6 when the planning session is complete. Each "producer" shares his/her plans within the group. Then, the group votes on which party would be the most interesting and exciting to attend.

3. Provide time for the winners from each group to present their plans to the entire class. The class then votes to determine which party would be the most exciting of all.

Party Producer

A PARTY FOR _____

Production plans and arrangements by:

_____

Description of Setting
or
Place for the Party: _____
_____
_____
_____

Guest List: _____ _____
_____ _____
_____ _____
_____ _____
_____ _____
_____ _____

Kind of cake: _____

Design of cake:
(Description or picture)

SPEECH MAKER'S WORKSHOP

Think of a project you would like your school or community to sponsor. In a single sentence, tell what the project is.

_____
_____
_____
_____

Now, write a radio speech (not to exceed 5 minutes) to explain the project. Remember to tell why you think your project would be good for the community. (Use the back of this page if you need more room.)

_____
_____
_____
_____
_____
_____
_____
_____
_____
_____
_____
_____
_____
_____
_____
_____
_____
_____

Speech Maker's Workshop

1. Read the speech to a friend.

2. Now, reread your speech. Underline the most important sentences.

3. Rewrite your speech using the underlined sentences. Try to limit the entire speech to 3 minutes. (Use the back of this sheet if necessary.)

_____
_____
_____
_____
_____
_____
_____
_____
_____
_____
_____
_____
_____
_____
_____
_____
_____
_____
_____
_____

Read the shorter speech to your friend, and ask your friend to answer these questions.
   1. Was something important left out?
   2. Which speech is more interesting?
   3. Which speech would be more apt to win community support for the project?

CLEM THE CLOD AND HIS ELOQUENT OWL

This is Clem the Clod,  and this  is his Eloquent Owl.

Clem is a talkative character who enjoys entertaining his friends with bits of gossipy information. However, since most of his friends are more refined than he, he depends on his friend, Eloquent Owl, to translate his coarse and often incorrect language into beautiful phrases.

Assist Eloquent Owl by translating and refining these statements that Clem has made.

"This here fat gal fell off her can and bopped herself on the beak." **(Example)** "This plump lady fell from her seat and injured her nose."

"Some kid was hanging around the corner with a face that looked like a pig had walked over it."

"She was a real ravel off the old bag with her hair smashed on her block and fancy stuff smudged all over her mug."

"That ole storm whupped that barn upside over and blew her clean across the state."

"He was so full-up with apple cider he cain't tell the difference among a bull and a barrel."

"He got hisself some new duds and pranced around like a peacock 'cross town to see his old lady."

MENACE MINIMIZED

To "minimize" is to reduce to the smallest possible amount, size, value, or degree. A person needs to know how to minimize, especially if he/she is to handle difficult situations.

Read each of the situations given below. Tell one or two things that might be done to minimize each problem.

A mother has three children aged 6, 8, and 12. Each child has invited one friend home after school. It could mean much confusion and a bad time for a mother and six children. What can the mother do to minize the potential trouble?

_____

_____

What might the children do to help minimize the problem?

_____

_____

An elderly neighbor's house has burned down, and he has nowhere to live. Dad has invited him to move in with the family for a few weeks. The neighbor has 7 cats. Your family hates cats. What can be done to minimize the problem?

_____

_____

It is the first day of school. The teacher has assigned seats in alphabetical order, and you are stuck next to a kid you just can't get along with. This person is a tease, and you anticipate a miserable year. Minimize!

_____

_____

HOW INVENTIVE ARE YOU?

PURPOSE: Inventing

PREPARATION
1. Reproduce the work sheets on the following pages.
2. Set aside a table or work area, and provide the following supplies: paste, scissors, felt pens, crayons, pencils, stapler and staples, stacks of the work sheets, and the study guide.

PROCEDURE

How Inventive Are You? Study Guide

1. Select the work sheet you want to do first.
2. Read the directions on the work sheet, and think about what you want to make before you begin.
3. Follow the directions on the work sheet.
4. Draw lines or add squiggles and squirms to complete your invention. Label it.
5. Continue until you have completed all four work sheets.
6. Use all the leftover shapes to design another invention. Label this invention, and state its purpose.
7. Make a mini-booklet out of your finished pages. Design and color a cover page, and staple it on top of your pages to complete your booklet.

How Inventive Are You?

Cut out these triangles. Paste as many as you need onto another sheet of paper to make something for a bird.

How Inventive Are You?

Cut out these circles. Paste as many as you need onto another sheet of paper to make an article of clothing.

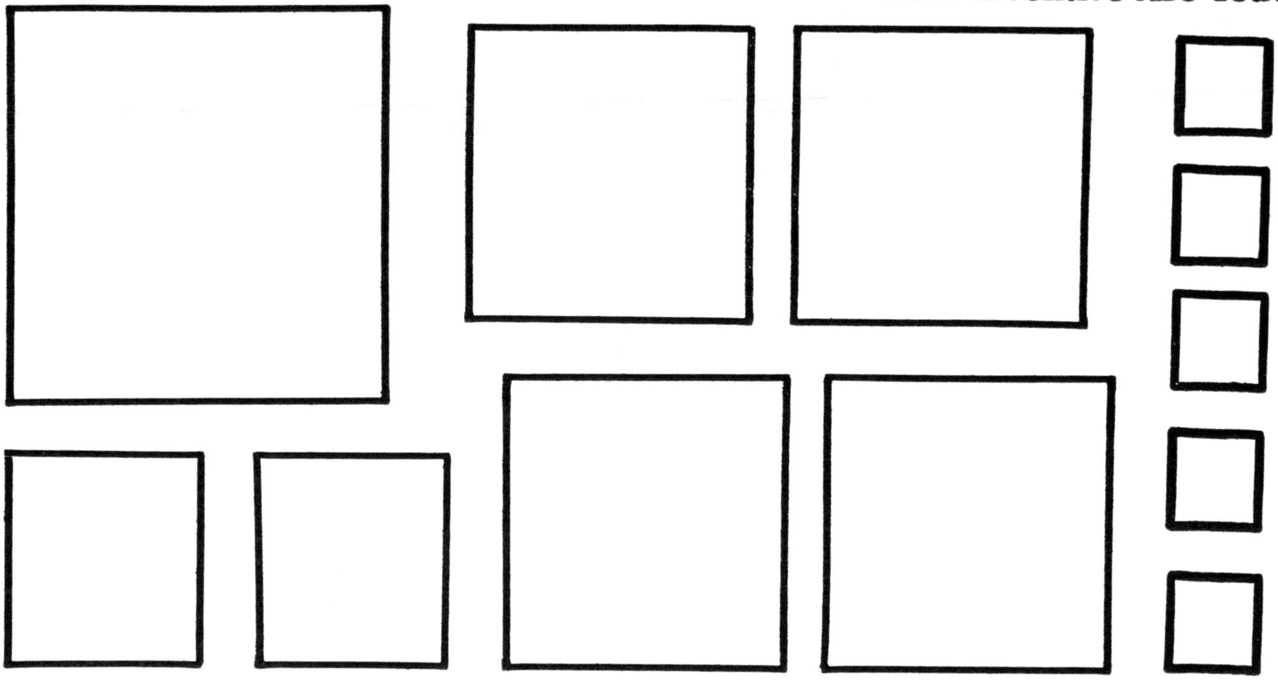

How Inventive Are You?

Cut out these squares. Paste as many as you need onto another sheet of paper to make a house.

164

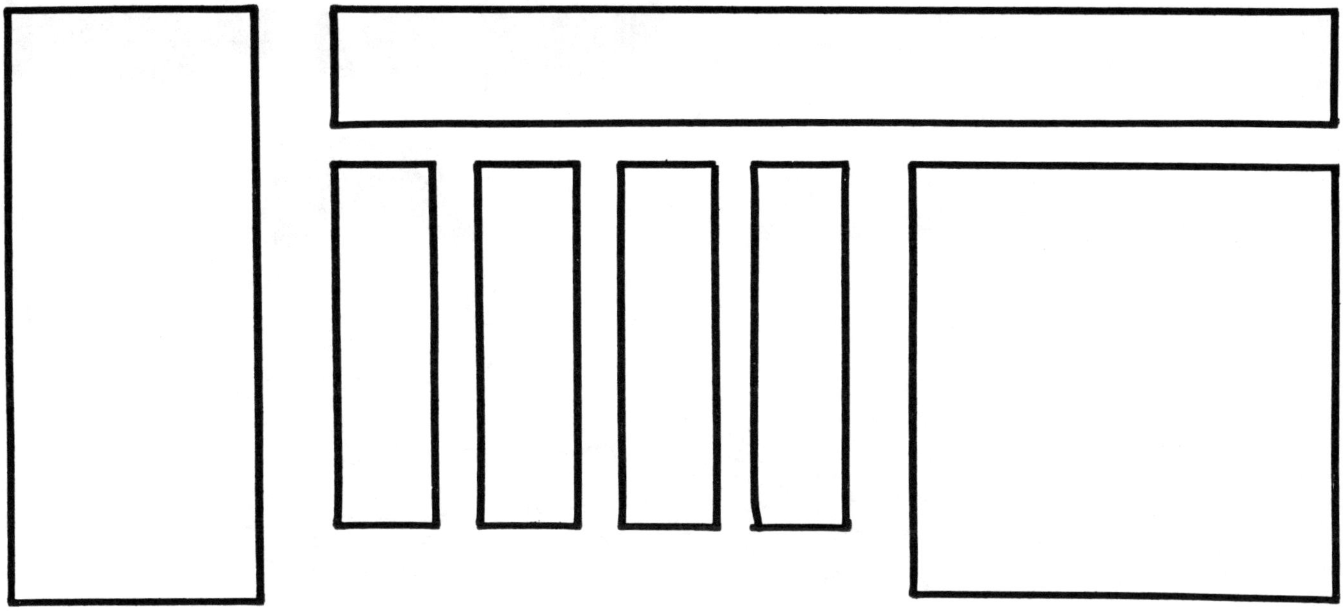

How Inventive Are You?

Cut out these rectangles. Paste as many as you need onto another sheet of paper to make a piece of furniture.

165

MAKE UP A MEASURE

PURPOSE: Inventing

PREPARATION
1. Read aloud to the students the story "The Blind Men and the Elephant."

PROCEDURE
1. Discuss how the handicap of blindness caused each man to approach the elephant with a distorted frame of reference.

2. Ask students to conjecture ways in which they could describe objects which could not be handled or felt to persons who cannot see (for example: a train, an acre, features of a person, a large monument, a lion,, etc.).

3. Divide students into groups of five or six, and ask them to suppose that there is no uniform system of measurement in existence. Given this problem, each group must devise a new and unique system for measuring height and length that could be used to describe the sizes of buildings, furniture, people, and household objects to someone who had never seen such objects.

4. After the groups have come up with a measurement system, they must plan a demonstration of the use of the new system.

5. Provide time for each group to share results of their thinking and demonstrate their system.

IMPROVEMENT, INC.

PURPOSE: Modifying

PREPARATION
1. Gather one or two objects from the following list for each of four to five groups of students.

ice cream cone	baseball mitt
bathroom scales	alarm clock
fork	pencil or pen
recipe box	wastebasket
small jewelry box	dictionary
empty billfold	barrette
coffee pot	toothbrush
white glue bottle	dollar bill
tape dispenser	box of cereal

2. Reproduce one copy of the following "Memo" for each group.

PROCEDURE
1. Divide students into four or five groups. Appoint a recorder for each group.

2. Direct students to brainstorm ideas for improvements on the object(s) given to their group. The recorder lists all ideas on a sheet of paper.

3. Students then agree on the improvements which should be included on a model drawing of the object as they would present it to the manufacturer. The recorder lists these on the "Memo" page, and another student (or students) makes the model drawing in the space provided on the "Memo" page.

Improvement, Inc.

MEMO

To the Manufacturers of: _____

From Members of IMPROVEMENT, INC.

_____ _____
_____ _____
_____ _____

Suggestions for improvement of afore-mentioned object.

1. _____   6. _____
2. _____   7. _____
3. _____   8. _____
4. _____   9. _____
5. _____   10. _____

DRAWING OF PROPOSED IMPROVEMENT:

Willy-Nilly Nomenclature

If you were not familiar with the Green Bay Packers, you might not guess that they were a football team. You might think they were a smoked fish market or a meat-packing company in Green Bay, or perhaps a large moving company.
Read this list of names that could have more than one identity.

Twice Told Tales	The Ponderosa	Yugoslavia	Babe Ruth
Great Emancipator	Yellowstone	G.I.	Hi Ho, Silver
Old Ironsides	Great Stone Face	Annapolis	R.S.V.P.
Virginia Woolf	Pensacola	Old Glory	C.O.D.
Headless Horseman	*The Wizard of Oz*	Big Ben	A.F.L.
Stonehenge	Saskatoon	Istanbul	V.I.P.

Choose 5 of these and write them in the first column below. Then, give at least three identities to each. (One must be correct.) Exchange papers with a friend, and put your mark by each correct identity given.

1.
2.
3.
4.
5.

PURPOSE: Maximizing

PREPARATION
1. Provide scissors, crayons, and a copy of the following two work sheets for each student.

PROCEDURE
1. Write the word "maximize" on the chalkboard and ask students to define it.

2. Distribute the work sheets. Allow time for students to read the information, verify the definition, and discuss it.

3. Direct students to follow the instructions on the work sheet. While students are working, ask these questions to stimulate new ideas for them.

   - In what ways could these animals be used as learning aids with first graders? (counting, adding and subtracting sets, learning names of animals, learning how animals are grouped in a real zoo, creating a zoo diorama, etc.)

   - In what ways could you use these animals? (as party place cards, invitations, room decorations, to make a mobile, bookmarks, etc.)

   - In what ways could a teacher or parent use the animal set?

   - How could the animals be used if they were magnified up to 5 or 6 times of the original size? (as posters, birthday cards, bulletin board decorations, advertising gimmicks, etc.)

Maximize a Menagerie

The word "maximize" means to make greater or to increase the value or use of something.

On these two pages, you will find a whole zoo of animals. Color them, and cut them out. Then fold them so that you can stand them up.

The most obvious uses for these paper animals are playing zoo or learning the names of the animals. Your job is to "maximize" the use of these animal cut-outs by thinking of at least 20 additional ways to use them.

While you are working, your teacher will ask some thought questions that may trigger new ideas for you. Write down your ideas on a sheet of paper, and be ready to share them with your classmates.

Maximize a Menagerie

Maria's Dilemma

PURPOSE: Inferring

PREPARATION:
1. Reproduce copies of the "Maria's Dilemma," "End-of-Story," and "Picture It" work sheets.

2. Lead a class discussion focused on inference skills. Make sure that all students understand the meaning of the term.

PROCEDURE
1. Distribute copies of the "Maria's Dilemma" work sheet, and ask students to read the story silently.

2. Discuss Maria's story in a group setting. Encourage students to express personal feelings related to Maria's family situation and her desire to visit her relatives in Iowa.

3. Ask students to underline the sentences as requested on the work sheet. Discuss the underlined sentences and their inferred meanings.

4. Use the "End-of-Story" and the "Picture It" work sheets as follow-up activities.

5. Share and compare story endings and pictures. Allow students to vote on the best ending and illustrations for the story.

MARIA'S DILEMMA

Maria is twelve years old. She lives in a big city in southern California with her mother, her aunt, and a younger brother. She is in the sixth grade and makes very good grades.

More than anything in the world, Maria wants to spend a summer vacation with her grandmother and cousins who live on a farm in Iowa. She has never seen these relatives, but they write warm, friendly letters and send birthday and Christmas presents every year to Maria and her family. They send snapshots, too, that show the big old house, the barn, the vegetable garden, the dog, and even the chickens and ducks. At night, Maria dreams of picking beans and tomatoes from the garden and gathering eggs from the hen house.

Maria's grandmother has written that she will send half the money for plane fare to Iowa if Maria can find a way to get the other half. Both Maria's mother and aunt want to help her, but neither of them have money to spare after the bills are paid. They work in a garment factory near the apartment where they live, and they try to work different shifts so one of them can be at home with the baby boy. Maria helps with the housework and plays with her brother as much as she can. Even though she wants to go to Iowa, she is not eager to be away from her own home for a whole summer, and she knows that getting the money will be a real problem.

Underline the two sentences that lead you to believe that Maria works hard.

Underline the sentence that leads you to believe that Maria's grandmother in Iowa wants her to come for a visit.

END-OF-STORY Maria's Dilemma

Think about some of the ways Maria's story could end.

How could Maria earn the money for half her plane fare to Iowa?
Could Maria take the train or bus instead, and use her grandmother's money for the full ticket?
If she took a baby-sitting job after school, how would this affect her mother, aunt, and brother?
What new experiences would be in store for Maria if she did arrange to spend the summer in Iowa?

Write one paragraph to give Maria's story an unhappy ending.

_____
_____
_____
_____
_____
_____
_____
_____
_____
_____

Now, write another paragraph to reverse the ending and make Maria happy.

_____
_____
_____
_____
_____
_____
_____
_____
_____
_____
_____

PICTURE IT   **Maria's Dilemma**

Finish this picture of Maria's home.

Draw the farm in Iowa. Show some of the people and animals.

176

Zany Authors

Read these directions aloud to yourself.

Have you read the book entitled *The Lost Correspondent* by Willie Everight? How about *Run for Your Life* by T. Rufus Falling? (Get it? If not, reread the paragraph.)

Below are 10 authors. Read their names carefully, and write an appropriate title for each one.

_____ by Ewell C. Gosts

_____ by U. R. Covert

_____ by I. Cara Lott

_____ by B. A. Moron

_____ by Willie Takit

_____ by M. Ike Razy

_____ by Lord Howitt Hurtz

_____ by Lou C. Goosey

_____ by Ima Lone

_____ by Oshee Bledsoe

Now, make up some titles and authors of your own. Have fun trying them on your friends.

_____ by _____

_____ by _____

_____ by _____

_____ by _____

PURPOSE: Conceptualizing

PREPARATION
1. Reproduce one copy of the following work sheet for each student.

PROCEDURE
1. Ask students to visualize the creation of a brand new city following the pattern of a giant web.

2. Direct students to use the web pattern on the work sheet to diagram the design and layout of these important elements in the new city.

3. After diagrams have been completed, instruct students to write on their diagrams the reasons for their placement of each element.

Housing   Schools   Religious Centers
Recreational Facilities   Government Facilities   Shopping Areas
Transit Systems   Business Centers   Industrial Areas

Web City

CRIMINAL AT LARGE

PURPOSE: Proposing and Designing

PREPARATION
1. Provide a sheet of poster-size paper or tag for each student.

2. Make a variety of colors in paint or crayons and scissors, rulers, and pencils available to the students.

PROCEDURE:
1. Ask students to work together to make a list of persons, places, ideas, emotions, and things that appear to be the cause of some misery in today's world. (Examples: cancer, greed, littering, prejudice, etc.)

2. When the list has been compiled, ask each student to chose one item and design a "Wanted" poster to be put in a public place to make people aware of this "criminal."

3. When posters have been completed, provide time for students to show their posters and share with the class a proposal as to what should be done to capture their "criminals."

4. Make arrangements to display posters in the hall or cafeteria where the ideas may be shared with other people.

Gala Gathering

You are the coordinator for a party to be held Friday afternoon. Approximately 35 people will attend. You have already decided on the menu you will serve (see the recipes on the following page.)

It is now Tuesday evening. You need to plan how you will manage the following details:

        grocery shopping
        table arrangements
        contacting and instructing hostesses who will serve
        time schedule for preparation

Use the following pages to show how you will organize your time and information. Before you get started, here are some things for you to consider.
1. How and when will I get the food ready?
2. Where can I get the things I need?
3. How long will it take to do the shopping?
4. How long will it take to contact all the hostesses?
5. How long will it take to gather trays, dishes, silverware, and other necessities?
6. How many people do I need to help serve?

Gala Gathering

POPCORN PUFFS
(makes 8 Puffs)

3 c miniature marshmallows
2 T butter
¼ t salt
food coloring (optional)
7 c popped corn
8 candy suckers

Place marshmallows, butter, and salt in top of double boiler and heat, stirring frequently, until mixture is smooth. (Add a few drops of food coloring if desired.) Pop corn and measure 7 cups into large buttered bowl. Pour hot mixture over corn and toss gently to coat. Quickly shape mixture into a 3" ball around each sucker. Cool before serving.

GREAT GRAPE GULP
(10-12 8 oz. servings)

1 6 oz. can frozen lemonade
1 6 oz. can frozen grape juice
1 6 oz. can frozen orange juice
4 c water
1 quart club soda
sugar to taste

Mix frozen ingredients with water and chill. Just before serving, add club soda and sugar to taste. Pour into glasses filled with crushed ice. Add purple grapes to each glass if desired.

FRUIT CRUNCHIES
(makes 36 1½" squares)

4 c crunchy cereal
1 3 oz. pkg. fruit-flavored gelatin
2 T butter
⅓ c corn syrup

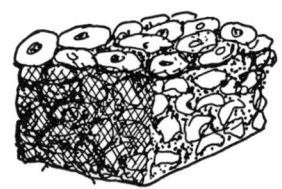

Mix butter, corn syrup, and gelatin in saucepan and bring to a boil over medium heat, stirring constantly. Remove from heat; stir in cereal, and pour into buttered 9" x 9" baking dish. Smooth top with buttered spoon. Cover and put in refrigerator for 45 minutes to set. Cut into 1½" squares.

BANANA POPS
(makes 16 Pops)

4 bananas
3 T butter
3 T milk
1 pkg. dry frosting mix
shredded cocoanut (toasted)
16 wooden lollipop sticks

Peel bananas and cut each into 4 sections. Insert a lollipop stick into each, and place on a waxed paper covered baking sheet in freezer for 2½ hours or until firm. Put butter and milk into double boiler. Melt butter and stir in frosting mix. Heat over boiling water for 5 minutes, stirring occasionally. Remove from burner. Dip banana pieces into mixture and roll in cocoanut. Set back on same baking sheet and chill (not freeze) until firm.

NOTE: Remember that you will need to expand your recipes to make enough food for all your guests. (You might plan to have a little left over!)

Gala Gathering

WHAT WILL I DO WHEN

Wednesday
- Morning:
- Afternoon:
- Evening: 

Thursday
- Morning: 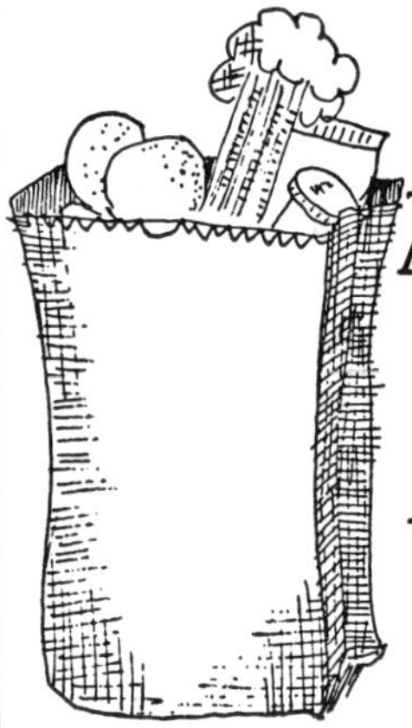
- Afternoon:
- Evening:

Friday
- Morning: 
- Afternoon:

SYNTHESIS COMPETENCY REVIEW

1. Read the sentence and circle the correct answer.

   If Nancy mowed her lawn in two hours last week, and in two hours and ten minutes the week before, you can infer that the task this week will take

   > about two hours
   > at least three hours
   > less than two hours
   > one hour

2. Read this sentence.

   She offered three kinds of ice cream to the children.

   Now, circle what you consider to be the most sensible hypothesis to be drawn from that sentence.

   > The dishes will not hold all the ice cream.
   > Different children like different kinds of ice cream.
   > The store has nine different kinds of ice cream.

3. Rearrange the words in this sentence to make a new one. Write your sentence on the lines below.

   A new student played the game.

   _____
   _____

4. Combine the six words below to form three compound words. Write your words on the lines.

dog	arm
fly	watch
chair	butter

   _____
   _____
   _____

5. Draw the patterns below in reverse order on the line below. Reverse the direction of each pattern as well as the order given.

   _____

6. Use these twelve shapes (and only these twelve shapes) to create a clown character. Try to keep each shape the exact size that it is shown. Draw your character in the circle below.

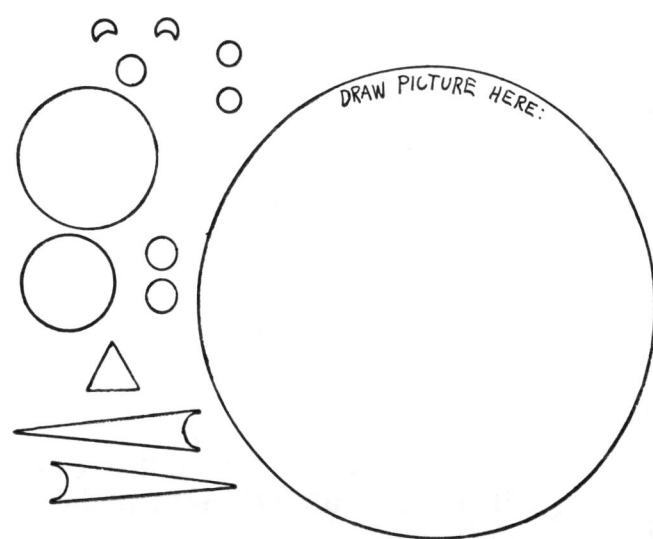

7. Rearrange the letters in each word to make a new one. Write your words on the lines.

   tub — _____
   ate — _____
   stop— _____

8. Using this code, write this message on the lines below.

   I am the real superhero.
   A = △   U = ⬓   P = ●
   E = ♡   T = ∞   S = ■
   I = ○   R = ▲   L = ▬
   O = □   H = ♥   M = ▰

   _____
   _____

9. Modify this sentence so that it includes at least two nouns, two adjectives, and two adverbs. Write your new sentence on the lines provided.

   The band played.

   _____
   _____

10. Draw a circle around the sentence that best demonstrates a refinement of the statement.

    Joe has a heap of troubles on his mind.

    Joe has many difficult problems to think about.
    Joe has a lot on his mind.
    Joe is unhappy

11. Choose the best substitute for the underlined word in each sentence from the list. Draw a line from each underlined word to its substitute.

	List
The house is <u>large</u>.	crazy
	silly
The lady is <u>pretty</u>.	enormous
	attractive
The book is <u>boring</u>.	abrupt
	dull

12. Read these three statements.

    A. Desert animals are most unusual.
    B. It's fun to get acquainted with sea creatures.
    C. Some animals enjoy winter weather.

    Now, read these sentences. In the blank before each, write the letter of the statement above upon which it expands.

    ____ Camels can carry water for weeks in their humps.
    ____ Starfish have dozens of tiny feet.
    ____ Stay away from an octopus, even a friendly one!
    ____ Sidewinder snakes scoot sideways across the sand.
    ____ Polar bears walk on ice without getting cold feet.
    ____ Scorpions dance when they mate.
    ____ Rabbits hop happily across snowy fields.
    ____ Penguins never get runny noses.
    ____ Did you ever see a giant pink lobster?

NOTE: *Many of the skills and processes presented in this section are best evaluated by more open-ended experiences than can be provided in a written competency review format. It is suggested that the teacher use the glossary as a guide to create additional evaluative activities similar to the models in the text.*

SKILL STUFF

EVALUATION

V. EVALUATION SKILLS AND PROCESSES — SKILLSTUFF Activities

- ___ Valuing
- ___ Predicting
- ___ Discussing
- ___ Selecting
- ___ Projecting
- ___ Conjecturing
- ___ Estimating
- ___ Rating
- ___ Criticizing
- ___ Deciding
- ___ Defending
- ___ Recommending
- ___ Disputing
- ___ Debating
- ___ Editorializing
- ___ Judging

PURPOSE: Valuing

PREPARATION
1. Make the label, "Something Important Is Happening Here," for a large box or basket.

2. Place the labeled container, drawing paper, and the study guide on the following page on a table easily accessible to the students.

PROCEDURE
1. Early in the morning, discuss the center *very briefly* with students. Guide the discussion to avoid student or teacher opinions or value judgments.

2. Make sure that the daily schedule is flexible enough to afford students plenty of time to complete the activity at their convenience. (Setting aside a period for this activity will turn it into a teacher-directed "assignment," and a portion of the student's personal commitment to the project will be sacrificed.)

3. On the following day, take the papers from the box and lead a discussion of the "important things." Avoid judgmental or critical appraisals of individual works. The focus on this activity should be on individual awareness and values, not on consensus.

4. Of course, you will want to close the initial discussion by telling students that your "important thing" is already in the box. They will surely want to know what's important to their teacher, and will eagerly await the "grand opening" of the box.

Something Important Is Happening Here

We sometimes get so involved in the routine of everyday living that we forget some of the really important things in our lives.

During your free time today, take out about fifteen or twenty minutes to think about just <u>one</u> thing in this classroom that is important to you that you really would not want to give up.

Take a sheet of paper from the table, and use your pencil, crayons, and/or pens to share this awareness with your classmates. Write a sentence, a paragraph, a poem, a song, a slogan, or a story; draw a picture; devise a cartoon, a brochure, a folder; or use any other creative medium you prefer. Feel free to sign your creation or leave it unsigned.

Fold your completed work, and place it in the "Something Important Is Happening Here" box. Tomorrow, we'll take the top off the box and find out more about ourselves and our classroom.

PREDICTION VISION

In each of the situations below, a decision needs to be made. Circle what you think is the best answer in each situation and tell why. Then tell what might happen if you made the wrong decision.

When I ride in a car, I always (fasten my seatbelt, hang out of the window).
Why? _____
Prediction: _____

When I go swimming, I always take along a (parakeet, friend).
Why? _____
Prediction: _____

When I cross the street, I (look both ways, run as fast as I can).
Why? _____
Prediction: _____

If I give someone a knife or a pair of scissors, I (pitch it to him, hand it to him carefully).
Why? _____
Prediction: _____

I always go down stairs (one at a time, by jumping from the top to the bottom).
Why? _____
Prediction: _____

CHERISH IS THE WORD

PURPOSE: Selecting/Discussing/Valuing

PREPARATION
1. Provide scissors, felt pens, and red construction paper for each student.

2. Prepare a large heart shape for the bulletin board.

PROCEDURE
1. Direct each student to cut out a large heart shape from red construction paper.

2. Ask each student to think of the five words in the English language that he/she loves most, and write these on the heart. Beside each word, the student must write one reason why that word was chosen.

3. Divide the class into groups of four or five, and allow students to share their word choices and reasons.

4. After all words and reasons have been shared, direct the groups to carry on a discussion session during which they must choose only five of all the words presented as the most important of all.

5. Reassemble the class, and discuss the choices of each group. Following the discussion, ask students to vote for the eight to ten words they care most about. Write these on the heart prepared for the bulletin board, and display for the class to enjoy.

HOW WOULD YOU FEEL?

Write one complete sentence to tell the world how you would feel if you were:

in a barrel headed over Niagara Falls.

a turkey the day before Thanksgiving.

the last person on earth.

winner of a one million dollar prize.

your country's head of state at the inagural ball.

caught with your hand in the cookie jar.

How Would You Feel?

a mouse being chased by a cat.

lost in the woods.

boarding a ship to sail around the world.

taking home a report card with all "A's."

the star of a TV show.

Now, go back and write one word in the box beside each sentence to sum up how you would feel.

Which best expresses the true feelings you think you would have, the complete sentence or the word?

Why do you think this is true?

NAME THE BUSINESS

The name of a business can make a lot of difference in how consumers think about it. Developers of shopping center complexes often spend a good deal of time and money coming up with just the right names to attract prospective customers to the businesses located in the center.

Think about this carefully. Then draw a line to match each of the ten businesses listed below with the best name for it. There are several possible choices for each, so test them out to get the very best name you can.

Lemon Tree	toy store
Century One	health food store
The Ware House	boating goods store
The Finishing Touch	tobacco shop
House of Art	health spa
Entertainment, Inc.	hotel
Ship Shape	disco/restaurant
Time of Your Life	cosmetics shop
New Look	clothing store
Midtown	delicatessen

Think of an entirely new name for one of the businesses, and make an attractive sign for it.

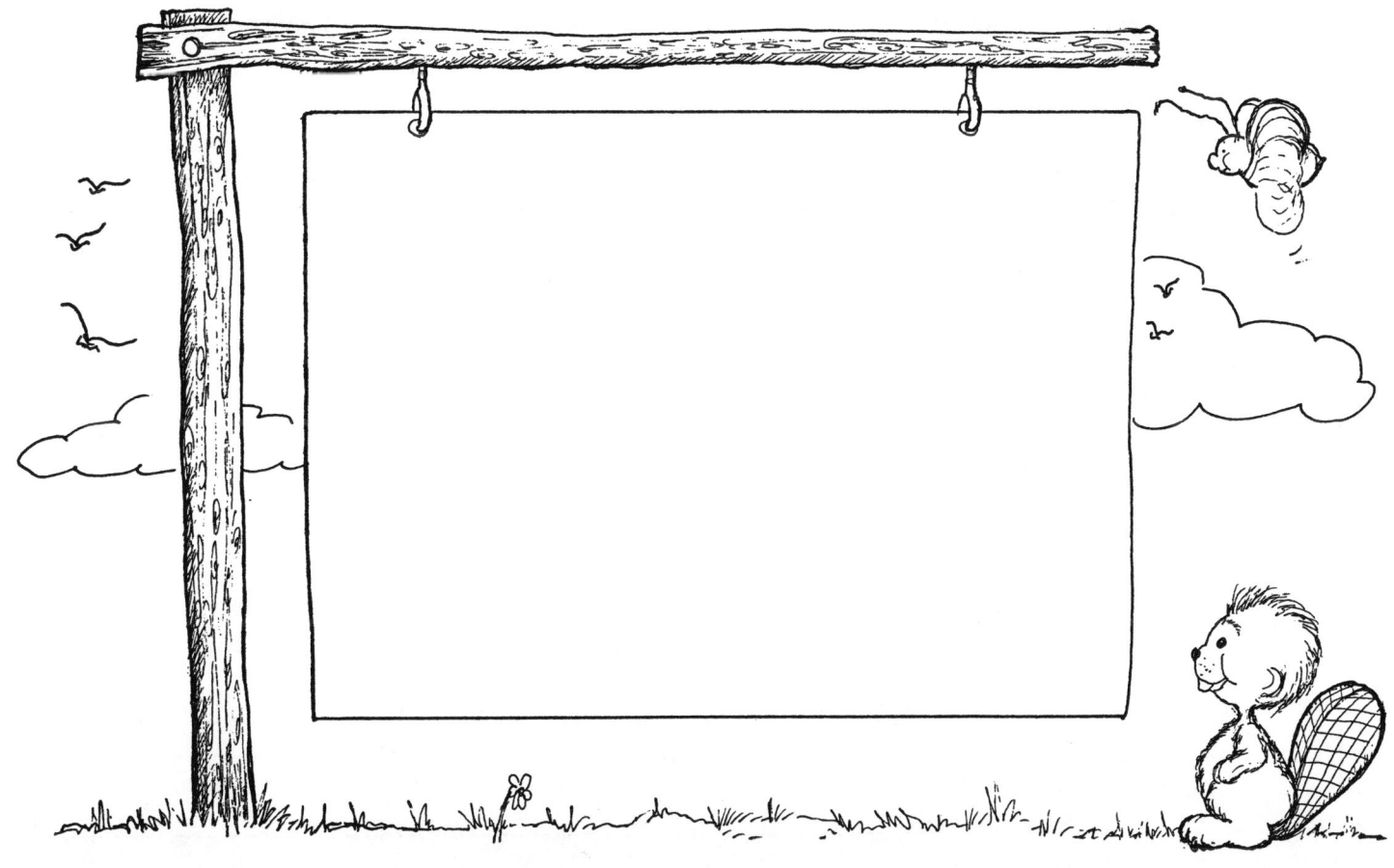

PERSONAL CAMOUFLAGE

PURPOSE: Conjecturing

PREPARATION
1. Provide old magazines, scissors, glue, pens, pencils, crayons, and colored construction paper for students to use.

PROCEDURE
1. Present this challenge to the class: "Compose a mystery statement about yourself that gives a hint as to your identity but does not disclose it."

   (For example, a boy who raises ducks might write, "I like chickens, but I love ducks." A red-headed girl might write, "Red is tops!")

2. Direct each student to write the statement on a piece of construction paper using any medium but his/her own handwriting. (Cut words from magazines, draw them rebus style, etc.)

3. Collect all statements, number them, and display them on a bulletin board.

4. Ask each student to number a piece of paper, read each statement carefully, and write his/her guess at that author's identify beside the appropriate number.

5. Provide time for students to share their guesses as well as their reasons for same.

ERNEST THE ESTIMATOR

Ernest knows that estimation is a useful and practical skill, one that he needs to use often in everyday life. He is trying to learn to estimate sums, products, differences, and quotients quickly.

List three things Ernest will need to estimate in each of the following situations.

Ernest is chairman of the refreshment committee for the Boy Scout Round-Up.

1. _____
2. _____
3. _____

Ernest has to do his homework and clean his room before he will be allowed to watch his favorite T.V. program, which is on at 8:00 p.m.

1. _____
2. _____
3. _____

Ernest wants to buy comic books, a felt pen, and a birthday present for his best friend with money he can earn by working after school.

1. _____
2. _____
3. _____

RATE YOUR READING

Rate the last three books you read. Consider:

- interesting plot
- attractive illustrations
- interesting writing style
- good character development

Rating Scale:
    1—excellent   2—good   3—fair   4—poor

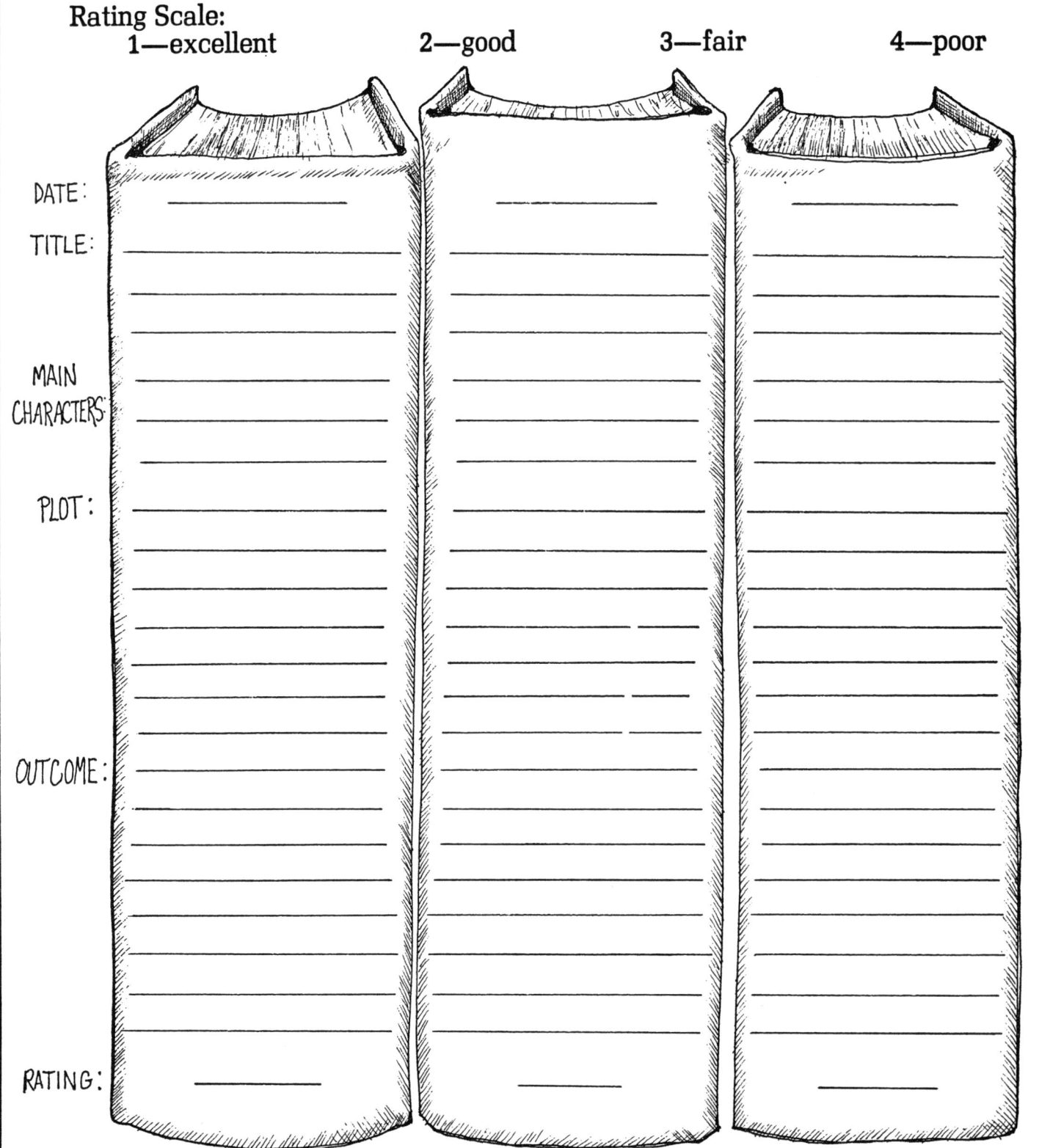

DATE:
TITLE:
MAIN CHARACTERS:
PLOT:
OUTCOME:
RATING:

CRITICALLY SPEAKING

Write a criticism of the book you gave the poorest rating on the "Rate Your Reading" chart. Try to be very specific.

Title _____

Author _____

Publisher _____

Copyright Date _____

Summary of Book _____

_____

_____

_____

_____

_____

Main Criticism _____

_____

_____

_____

_____

The book could have been improved by _____

_____

_____

PRINCIPAL POWER

A school principal's life is not always easy. Have you ever thought about how many important decisions have to be made in the school principal's office every day?

Put yourself behind the principal's desk, and test your power to think like a principal.

1. What would be the three most important things for you to do the week before school starts?

   1)_____

   2)_____

   3)_____

2. What would be your three major concerns on the first day of school?

   1)_____

   2)_____

   3)_____

Principal Power

3. Put a check beside the groups you would involve in making school rules.
   ____ the parents
   ____ the students
   ____ the teachers

   Rank the influence you think those groups should have on school rules in order, with #1 showing the group that should have the most influence.

   #1

   #2

   #3

4. Write a three-sentence description of your job as principal.

5. What would be your single most important task?

6. List 5 important talents, abilities, or character traits that would help you make good decisions.

EXPLANANATION IN ORDER

PURPOSE: Projecting

PREPARATION
1. Reproduce the "Explanation In Order" cards on the following two pages. Cut them apart and paste on index cards. (Add more of interest to your own group.)

2. Put the cards in a file box or letter file, and place them in a free choice activity center.

3. Provide the following directions.

PROCEDURE
1. Read through the cards and select one situation that you feel you could picture yourself in.

2. Ask a classmate to play the role of the person you would "explain to." Role play the situation to help you find out how you would actually handle it.

Explanation in Order

You promised to be home by 4:30 p.m. You were playing with a friend, the time slipped away, and you arrived at your own front door at 6:30 p.m. instead.

To whom will you make your explanation?
How will you explain?
What do you think the consequences will be?

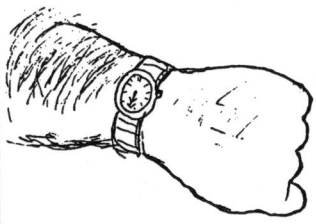

You forgot all about your homework assignment. You remembered it just as you walked into the classroom.

To whom will you make your explanation?
How will you explain?
What do you think the consequences will be?

You promised to clean up your own room before going to bed last night, but you were so sleepy and tired that you just didn't keep your promise. You are already late for school and can't do it now.

To whom will you make your explanation?
How will you explain?
What do you think the consequences will be?

You left your best jacket outside over night. It rained all night, and your jacket is faded and completely out of shape.

To whom will you make your explanation?
How will you explain?
What do you think the consequences will be?

Explanation In Order

You have lost a library book that is very popular with other members of your class. You know that it is the only copy in your school library. You have looked and looked, but it is nowhere to be found.

To whom will you make your explanation?
How will you explain?
What do you think the consequences will be?

You accepted a part in the school play and attended play practice three times. You hate the part, and you don't want to memorize the lines. It really is too late for someone else to accept the part now, but you want out anyway.

To whom will you make your explanation?
How will you explain?
What do you think the consequences will be?

You are chairman of a science committee responsible for planning the school science fair. You wanted to be chairman, but you just can't get the other members of the committee to work. Your committee report is due, and it just isn't ready.

To whom will you make your explanation?
How will you explain?
What do you think the consequences will be?

You saved enough money to buy holiday gifts for the members of your family and your best friend. When you went shopping for the gifts, you saw a jacket you wanted so badly you spent all the money you had for it. Now, gift giving time is here, and you have no gifts to give.

To whom will you make your explanation?
How will you explain?
What do you think the consequences will be?

IN DEFENSE OF A CHAIR

This is a chair!

No, this is a chair.

No, this is a chair.

No, this is a chair.

No, this is a chair.

WHAT IS A CHAIR? Is it a piece of furniture on which one sits? Well, then this could be a chair!
No?

Then, what is a CHAIR?

Write your own definition of a chair, and defend it by explaining why all the above are chairs, and why other pieces of furniture are not.

A CITIZEN SPEAKS!

Think of an appropriate proposal for one of the following changes.

1) A new name for your state
2) A new name for your school
3) A new method for electing a mayor, president, or prime minister
4) A new position in your city, county, state, or national government

Choose one of these and use this form to write your recommendation to the appropriate authority.

From: _____
(your name)
_____
(your address)
_____
(City, State, Zip)

To: _____
(Name)
_____
(Address)
_____
(City, State, Zip)

A Proposal Concerning: _____
_____

Recommendation: _____
_____
_____
_____

SAY IT ISN'T SO!

Each of the above statements is an advertising slogan used by a major American company. Each is designed to create in the consumer a particular feeling about the product it is trying to sell. Ask yourself these two questions about each of the statements:
1. What is the intention of the statement?
2. What could possibly be untrue about the statement?

Use the spaces below to dispute each statement by listing two situations in which the statement may not be true. Then, rewrite the statements to make them more realistic.

TAKE A POSITION

PURPOSE: Debating

PREPARATION
1. Provide a copy of the following work sheet for each student.

PROCEDURE
1. Direct each student to read the work sheet carefully and determine which position he/she can defend most honestly.

2. Divide the class into two teams of like persuasions. Provide time for teams to meet and discuss their ideas.

3. Ask each team to keep notes on points favoring that side of the issue.

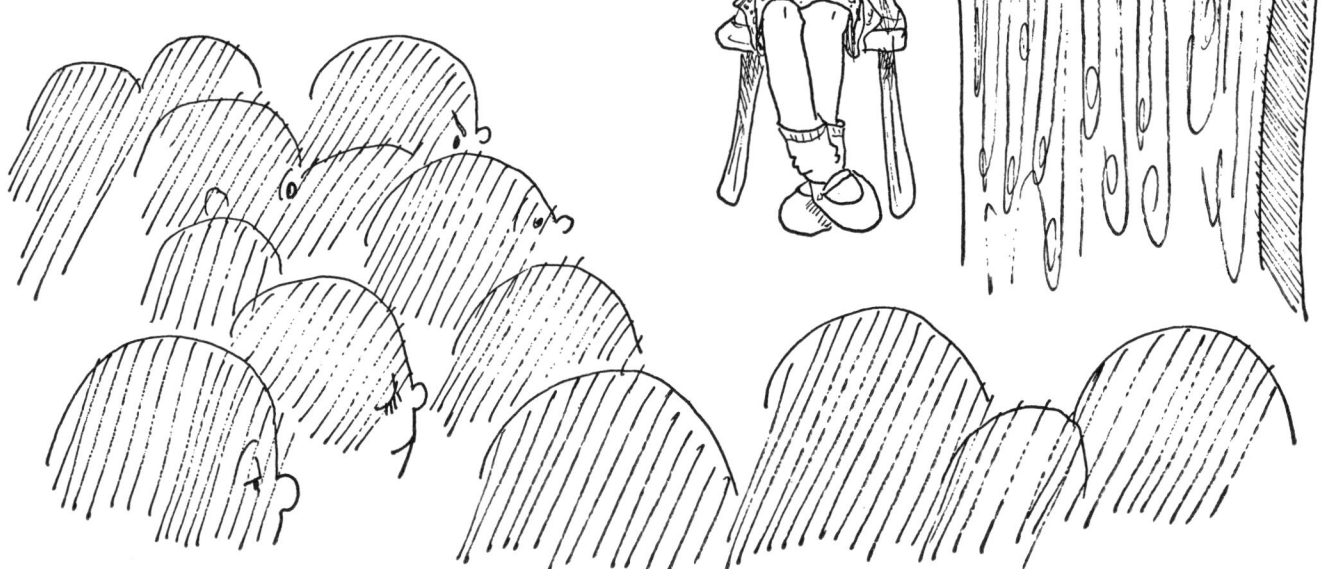

4. Ask each team to appoint two members of the group as representatives to sit on a panel of "expert debators."

5. Stage a debate in which the debators present, refute, and defend their positions.

208

Take a Position

Television, as an efficient source of information, a vehicle for vicarious experience, or a smorgasbord of ideas and ideals, makes more of a POSITIVE than a negative contribution to successful living.

Television, as a "hypnotist of the mind," a creator of unrealistic goals and desires (especially in advertising), and as a medium which breeds indolence and non-participation, makes more of a NEGATIVE than a positive contribution to successful living.

You must choose to support one of the above statements. Which will you choose?

To help you decide, ask yourself these questions:

1. How much time do you and your family members spend watching TV?
2. What are the reasons you watch TV?
3. In what good ways has TV affected your life?
4. What bad effects has TV had on you?
5. In the near future, TV may be used as an instrument for actually looking into your home—asking questions and tabulating your responses. How could that affect your life?

Newspaper Know-How

PURPOSE: Editorializing

PREPARATION
1. Reproduce a copy of the "Newspaper Know-How" information sheet on the following page for each student.
2. Print the Procedure directions on a chart or study guide.
3. Provide pencils, paper and newspapers for the students.
4. Place all materials in a free-choice interest center for individual student use, or use as a homework assignment.

PROCEDURE
1. Follow the Study Guide directions.

STUDY GUIDE
Read both articles on the "Newspaper Know-How" information sheet. Then answer the following questions on a separate piece of paper.
1. What is the difference between a fact and an opinion?
2. How is a news article different from an editorial?
3. Underline the facts in the news article, and write a short summary of them.
4. What is the major concern of the editorial?
5. Underline the one sentence in the editorial that best sums up the author's opinion.
6. Why do you think that a news article is not supposed to contain opinions?
7. Should an editorial contain facts? Why or why not?
8. Do you think editorials are good things to have in newspapers? Why or why not?
9. If you had all the facts about a news event, and an opinion about the event, would you rather write a news article or an editorial? Why?
10. Select a news article from a paper in the center. Write an editorial giving your opinion of the situation or event discussed in the article. Copy the article on another sheet of paper, and display your article and editorial.

Daily Banner
15¢

NEW SCHOOL BOARD MEMBERS APPROVED

A slate of nine new School Board members, selected by Mayor H. Freeman and offered to the Roswell Metropolitan City Council for approval, was accepted as presented by the necessary 2/3 majority vote at the City Council meeting held May 21, 1980 at the Roswell City Courthouse. The meeting was attended by the Mayor and Council members. Although the public was informed of this open meeting, no representatives from the private sector were present.

The nine new Board members are Kathy Ci, James Schwinn, Elva McMahon, L. G. Mimms, Helen Hampton, C. R. Bishop, Jacob Wilbur, O. T. Harper and Nan Cahn. The new members will assume their responsibilities on August 1, 1980, when current members will have finished their terms. Members sit on the board for four years, and hold two open meetings every month to review, discuss and decide on city-wide school policies and problems. No fiscal compensation is granted to board members.

IT SEEMS TO ME
BY MAGGIE UPSON-DOWNS

It seems that the news media's major brou-ha-ha concerns our nation's public schools. Kids can't read; teacher's can't maintain discipline; principals don't support teachers, and the public is in an uproar over the astronomical amounts of tax dollars 'wasted' on 'non-academics.' Public schools are being deserted by almost anyone who can afford the cost of private education.

Could one cause be apathy? It seems unlikely when one considers the amount of words in the media about the matter. But think about what is said — outcries about the effects. Public school policy decisions are made by the School Board, which is selected by the Mayor and approved by the City Council. Only yesterday, a new slate of Board members was voted on by the Council. The meeting was an open one, well-publicized in advance. How many private citizens attended? Ten? No. Five? Guess again. Zero is the correct amount. There are over 70,000 students in our public school system, and not one parent or guardian showed up to voice any opinion about the people who make the decisions that affect their children's daily lives.

If parents — and the public in general — are unhappy with the results of their children's education, it seems to me that they should participate in the submission of candidates' names, and be present to make their feelings known when the slate is voted on.

It's too late to complain when the voting is over and the people are in office. It's too late to complain when decisions have been made and programs set. It's much too late when effects are already showing up.

So do something about it before everything is settled. Get off your apathy and make your feelings known!

NUKE OR NOT?

Deciding on the best solution to a real life problem can be very difficult because the alternatives to consider often have both advantages and disadvantages. In order to make the decision that is best and most fair for all concerned, one must weigh the advantages of each alternative against the disadvantages.

One good example of this kind of problem is **whether or not a nation should develop the use of nuclear power for domestic purposes.**

Listed below are some of the advantages and disadvantages of nuclear power. Use all the resources available to you to add to these lists. (You may wish to subtract some if you find that you disagree with them.)

ADVANTAGES	DISADVANTAGES
1. Nuclear power is plentiful.	1. Nuclear power is a threat to personal safety.
2. Nuclear power is cheap.	2. Nuclear power can be a threat to national security.
3. Nuclear power is versatile.	

_____   _____
_____   _____
_____   _____
_____   _____
_____   _____

When you have made each list as complete as possible, pretend that you are the person with final authority to make the decision. State your decision, and give your rationale on the lines below.

DECISION: _____
_____
_____
_____

EVALUATION COMPETENCY REVIEW

Read the statements below.

   A. "His approach was much too radical to appeal to such a conservative audience."
   B. "If it rains, the spectator attendance at the ballgame will be much lower than normal."
   C. "Mt. Shasta is about a three-day car trip from Chicago."
   D. "In math he demonstrates superior skill, but he is poor in athletics."
   E. "You have vanilla, chocolate, and strawberry? I would like strawberry, please."
   F. "You are committing an immoral act if you vote to promote the further development of nuclear power."
   G. "Rather, I would advise you not to vote at all."
   H. "If you like strawberries, you'll love my parfait recipe."
   I. "The baby weighs approximately nine pounds.
   J. "It is more important to be a good friend than to be popular."
   K. "I would imagine that the president of a country is at times overcome with loneliness and anxiety."
   L. "If the water level has risen 4 inches in 10 rainy days, and we are expecting 5 more rainy days, we can probably expect the water level to exceed a total of 6 inches."
   M. "The end justifies the means."
   N. "But he had to present the radical view in order to motivate those people to action against the opposing party."
   O. "A much-needed and very exciting political analysis was made by an attractive supporter who spoke in well-modulated tones with great authority."

Refer to these statements as you read the following questions. Circle the correct answer for each.

1. An American presidential candidate once said, "I would rather be right than be president." His values would probably most closely match those of

   speaker H
   speaker K
   speaker J

2. Statement L could most accurately be described as a

   judgment
   estimate
   prediction

3. Which speaker is making a documented projection as to a future occurrence?

   speaker B
   speaker C
   speaker H

4. The statement which best demonstrates the process of selection is

   statement G
   statement E
   statement M

5. The two statements which best demonstrate an element of conjecture are

> statements B and I
> statements K and M
> statements K and H

6. Estimates are made by

> speakers C and I
> speakers C and D
> speakers J and I

7. A rating process is being employed by

> speaker D
> speaker J
> speaker E

8. Statement A could most accurately be labeled

> a criticism
> a conjecture
> a recommendation

9. Statements F and G place the person to whom they were directed in the position of having to

> editorialize
> estimate
> decide

10. Which statement is a direct defense of statement A?

> statement O
> statement G
> statement N

11. The strongest example of judgment is demonstrated in

> statement F
> statement C
> statement K

12. A man who loves whole strawberries, but hates cream in any form would be likely to dispute which statement?

> statement H
> statement M
> statement J

13. Which statement would most likely provide the best basis for a heated debate?

> statement B
> statement F
> statement J

14. The statement which is the best example of editorial writing is

> statement J
> statement L
> statement O

15. The statement which makes a strong recommendation in response to a prior statement is

> statement H
> statement G
> statement J

NOTE: *Many of the skills and processes presented in this section are best evaluated by more open-ended experiences than can be provided in a written competency review format. It is suggested that the teacher use the glossary as a guide to create additional evaluative activities similar to the models in the text.*

SKILLSTUFF

Answer Key & Glossary

REASONING

ANSWERS FOR COMPETENCY REVIEWS

I. Comprehension
1. S, T
2. skating
3. November
4. 9
5. 18
6. 3
7. the photographer
8. elderly man
9. At which stop did you get on this bus?
10. Ask the bus driver.
11. reading about busses in the encyclopedia
12. a bus driver's hat
13. C

II. Application
1. 4-6-8-9
2. A and C
3. 6, 9, 4, 1
4. A
5. A
6. 3, 1, 4, 2
7. wall
8. Accept any answer that fits.
9. Behave nicely
10. Joining one group of items to another group of items to obtain a total number of items
11. raging
12. I. Babies
    A. Characteristics
       1. Affectionate
       2. Dependent
       3. Demanding
       4. Often wet
       5. Always hungry

III. Analysis
1. those holding an object or wearing some equipment
2. less than half of them
3. The lady in high heels has the largest hat. The space creature and the scuba diver are taller than the boy.
4. four
5. a group of five and a group of two
6. Everyone but the driver would share a seat.
7. the lady in the polka dot dress
8. the snorkle is to the scuba diver.
9. the tall man's legs and the baby's legs
10. "What do you do for fun and relaxation?"
11. The lady should go on a diet.
12. "A smashing, humorous poster of seven unique characters."
13. peacock
14. Most of the characters are wearing something on their heads. Very few of the characters have on watches.

IV. Synthesis
1. about two hours
2. Different children like different kinds of ice cream.
3. A student played the new game.
4. watchdog; butterfly; armchair
5. [drawings]
6. Accept any arrangement that resembles a human form.
7. but; tea; post or spot
8. ○ △■■ ☊♡♡ ▲♡△■■ ■☐●♡▲♥♡▲☐
9. Answers will vary.
10. Joe has many difficult problems to think about.
11. enormous; attractive; dull
12. A; B; B; A; C; A; C; C; B

V. Evaluation
1. speaker J
2. prediction
3. speaker B
4. statement E
5. statements K and H
6. speakers C and I
7. speaker D
8. a criticism
9. decide
10. statement N
11. statement F
12. statement H
13. statement F
14. statement O
15. statement G

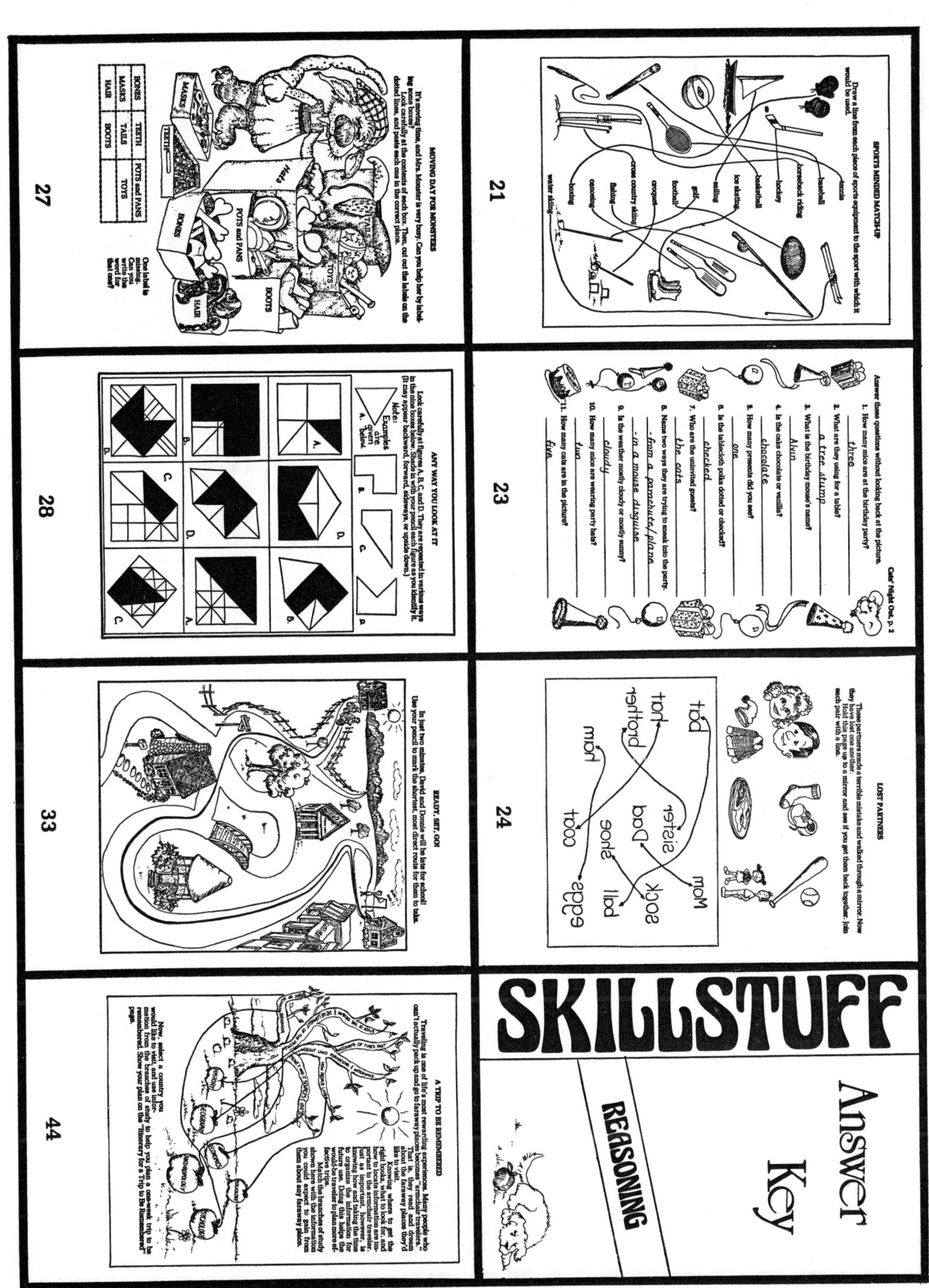

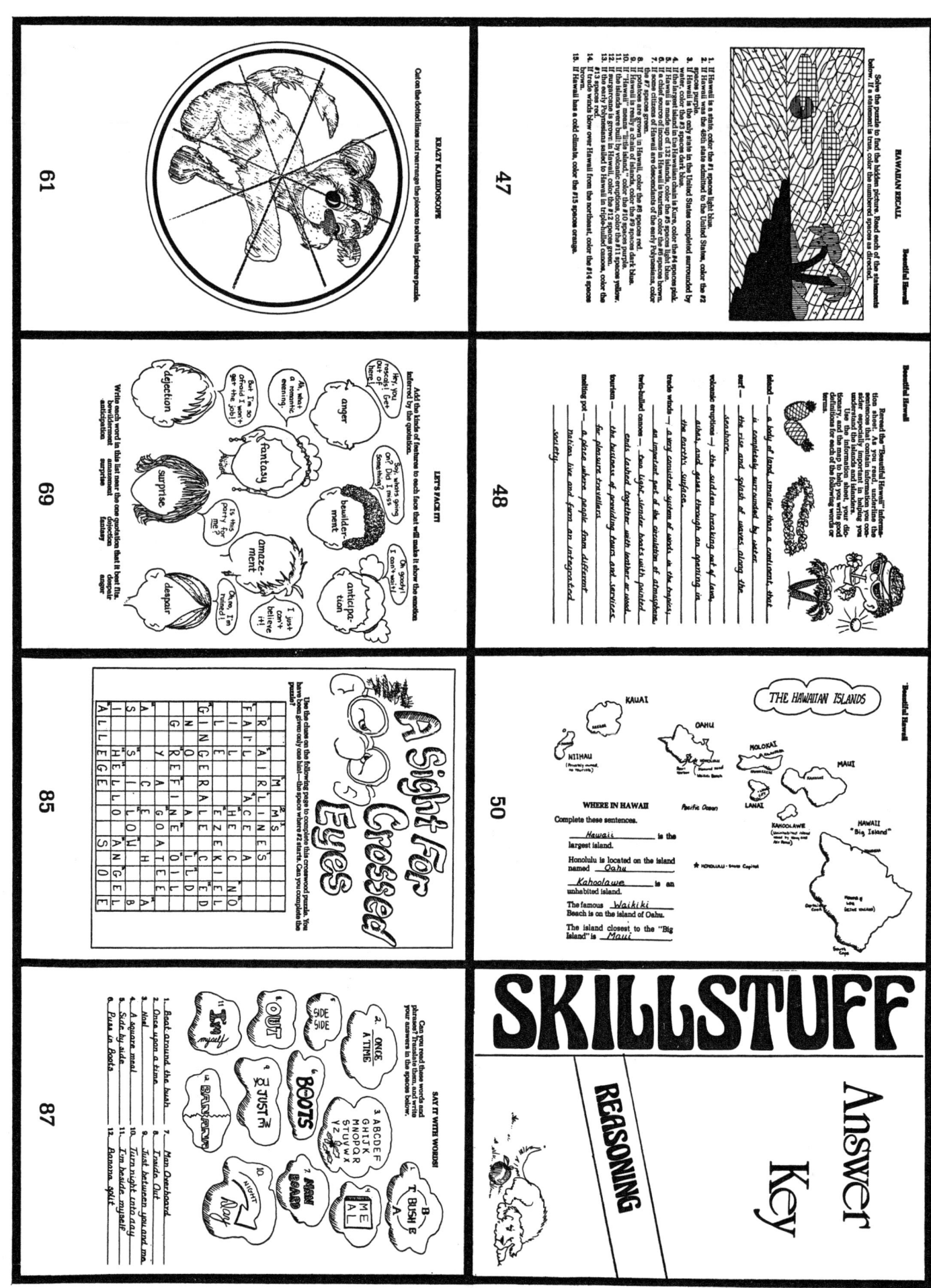

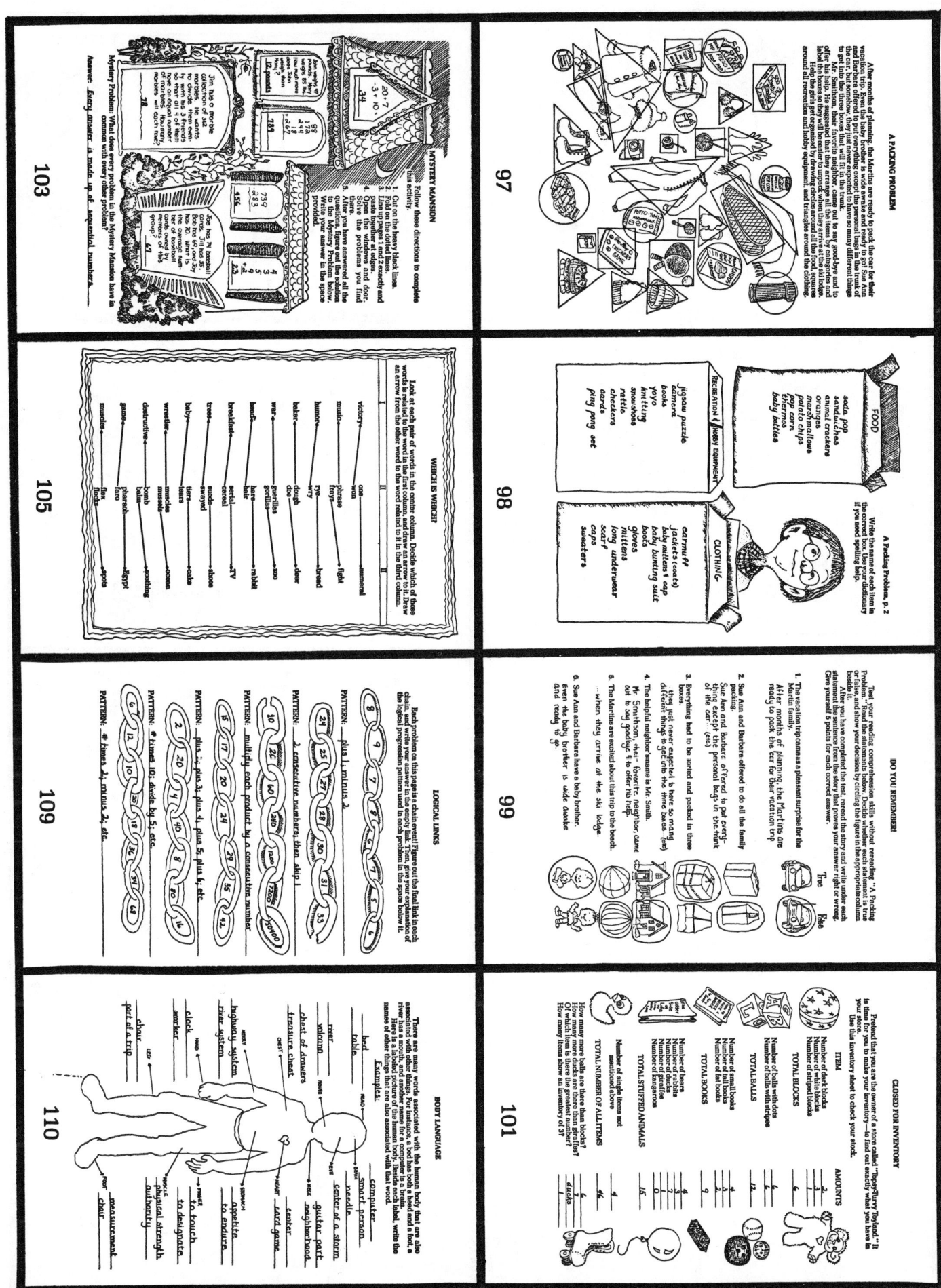

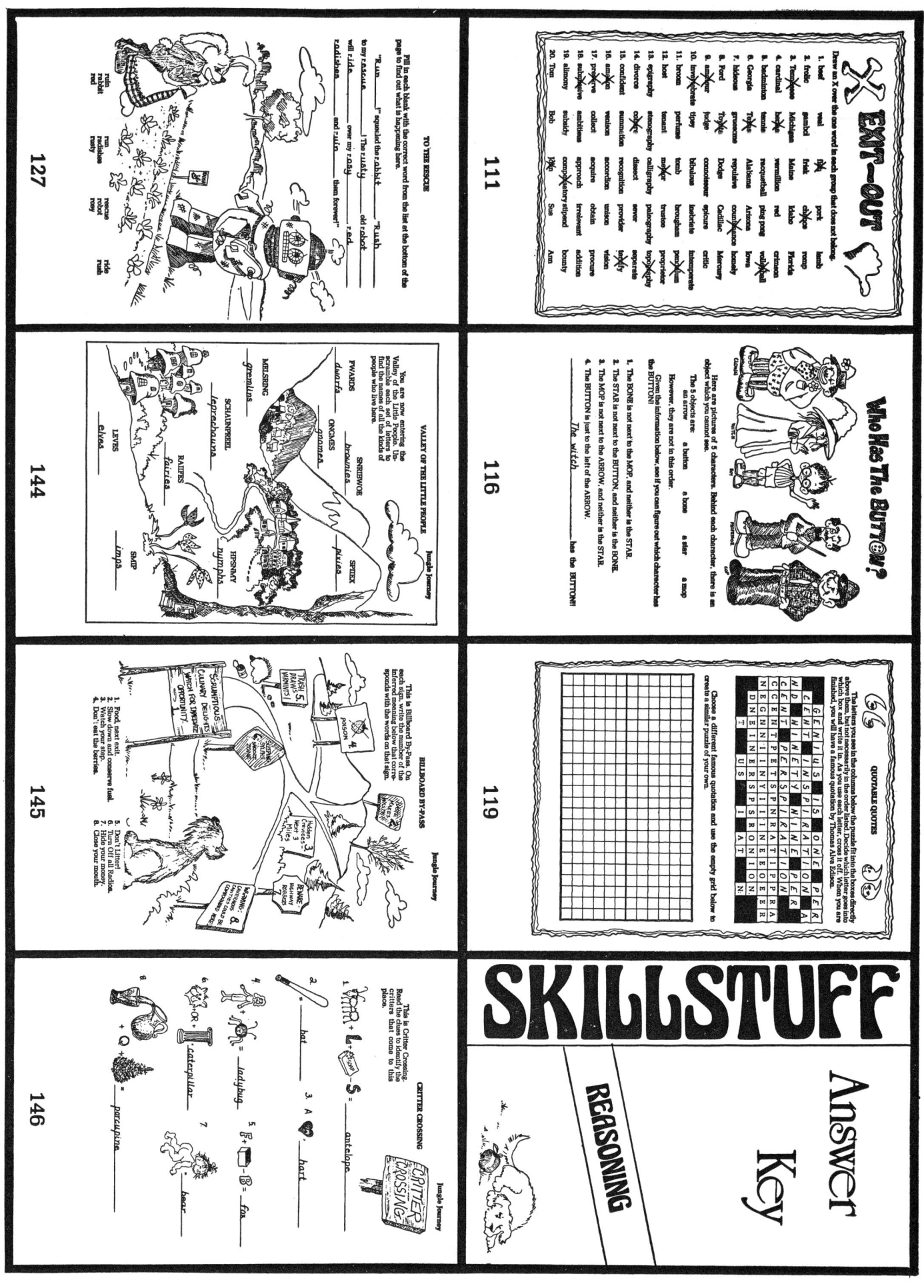

GLOSSARY OF SKILLS AND PROCESSES

COMPREHENSION—recalling and recognizing information and/or translating that information into a different symbolic form of language.

Skills and Processes Which Require **COMPREHENSION:**

Collecting—gathering or assembling items that meet a given standard or criteria.

Defining—explaining the meaning of a term set forth.

Describing—telling about something in detail.

Discovering—arriving at new knowledge through study, experiment, or research.

Identifying—to define or ascertain the definitive qualities of something.

Labeling—classifying, describing, or designating for identification purposes.

Listening—applying one's self to hearing something.

Locating—finding by searching, examining, or experimenting.

Matching—showing the correspondence between two items that are either alike or have corresponding qualities.

Observing—systematic watching.

Questioning—inquiring in a manner that will result in the acquisition of desired information.

Reading—gaining information from written or printed matter.

Recalling—remembering an experience or information.

Researching—systematic investigation of resources related to a given topic or idea.

Responding—reacting to a given stimulus.

APPLICATION—making use of knowledge gained and understood in dealing with new, concrete problems or situations.

Skills and Processes Which Require **APPLICATION:**

Arranging—placing in a deliberate order according to some criteria.

Assembling—joining or fitting together the parts to make the whole.

Associating—joining in a relationship; connecting in the mind or in the imagination.

Brainstorming—searching for all kinds of ideas related to a given problem or situation; usually done in a group setting.

Constructing—forming by the systematic assembling of parts.

Demonstrating—illustrating or explaining by practical application.

Diagramming—making a labeled plan, chart, or drawing of something.

Dramatizing—adapting for presentation by actors, as in a play.

Experimenting—conducting tests to demonstrate a truth or to examine the validity of an hypothesis.

Explaining—interpreting; giving reasons for and analyzing causes of.

Illustrating—making clear by a picture, diagram, or an example.

Interpreting—clarifying the meaning of something.

Interviewing—obtaining information by means of a personal question-and-answer session between an interviewee and a questioner.

Listing—recording a series of things.

Outlining—putting summarized information into an organized format which uses Roman numerals, capital letters, regular integers, and lower case letters to designate the relative importance of each item.

Recording—registering information in writing or in another permanent form.

Reporting—presenting a formal account or summation of a body of information.

Scheduling—making a planned program of events in timetable format.

Sequencing—arranging in logical order of ocurrence.

Simulating—creating an imitation of a real object or experience.

Sketching—creating a verbal or pictorial informal representation of an object or an experience.

Surviving—remaining in existence.

Translating—expressing something in a different style or medium from that in which it was originally presented.

ANALYSIS—separating information; taking apart the unknown; studying a problem in light of conscious knowledge of its parts and their relationships.

Skills and Processes Which Require **ANALYSIS:**

Abstracting—considering theoretically qualities or attributes without reference to a particular tangible example or object.

Advertising—making public announcement of; attracting attention to the qualities of a product or service.

Calculating—ascertaining the answer to a problem by computation.

Categorizing—arranging according to classes or a system of classification.

Comparing/Contrasting—examining in terms of similarities and differences (comparing focuses on similarities; contrasting stresses differences).

Decoding—converting from code into plain (normally understood) text.

Dissecting—separating in order to analyze, examine, or criticize in detail.

Differentiating—discriminating or perceiving the difference between kinds of things.

Generalizing—forming a concept or conclusion inductively from many particulars.

Inventorying—surveying by means of a detailed list.

Relating—making logical or natural associations among given items.

Separating—sorting by discrimination; isolating.

Solving—working out the correct solution to a given problem.

Surveying—making a detailed inspection or comprehensive viewing of.

SYNTHESIS—putting together new information; solving a problem through original, creative thinking.

Skills and Processes which Require **SYNTHESIS:**

Combining—bringing into a state of unity; merging; blending.

Composing—making or creating by putting together parts or elements.

Conceptualizing—formulating an original theory or idea.

Creating—causing to exist; originating.

Designing—conceiving a plan for; inventing.

Encoding—translating a message from plain language into a new system of symbols, letters, or words which have been assigned arbitrary meanings for that particular system.

Extending—broadening or expanding something to make it more comprehensive or inclusive.

Formulating—expressing in systematic terms or concepts; devising or inventing.

Hypothesizing—making an assertion subject to verification or proof.

Imagining—creating in the mind; conjecturing through mental imagery.

Inferring—concluding from evidence; deducing.

Inventing—devising first.

Magnifying—making greater in size or importance; amplifying.

Maximizing—increasing to make use of the greatest possible value or potential of something.

Minimizing—reducing to the least possible degree.

Modifying—altering the form or character of something.

Organizing—bringing information together into a structured state.

Producing—creating and presenting a product or service made by mental or physical effort.

Proposing—presenting an idea or a plan of action for discussion or adoption.

Rearranging—modifying a given plan or order of a group of elements, thus changing the perspective of the whole or the relationship of the parts.

Refining—using precise distinctions in thought or speech.

Reversing—changing to an opposite position, condition, or direction.

Substituting—replacing an original element with another of like or appropriate character.

Summarizing—presenting the main points in condensed form.

Visualizing—forming a mental image or picture of.

EVALUATION—making qualitative or quantitative judgments according to self-made or given criteria and as a result of logical thinking.

Skills and Processes Which Require
EVALUATION:

Conjecturing—inferring from inconclusive evidence; guessing.

Criticizing—reviewing the merits and faults of a given product or performance through some form of commentary.

Debating—engaging in a formal discussion or argument over opposing points of view.

Deciding—concluding or making a judgment through careful consideration of all pertinent matters.

Defending—justifying by action or argument.

Discussing—speaking with others in an effort to reach agreement, to convince, or to ascertain a truth.

Disputing—debating; questioning the validity of.

Editorializing—presenting a situation from a personal perspective; slanting objective information toward a personal bias.

Estimating—calculating approximately; forming a tentative opinion.

Judging—carefully appraising a problem or a situation, citing advantages, limitations, consequences, and implications.

Predicting—foretelling the outcome of a situation.

Projecting—transporting in one's imagination; imagining a plan or a intention for.

Rating—ranking or grading.

Recommending—advising adoption of a choice; citing favorable characteristics and qualifications or advantages over other possible choices.

Selecting—choosing from among several that which is preferable.

Valuing—rating in terms of usefulness or importance to the evaluator.

REASONING

TABLE OF CONTENTS

- SOME COMMON SENSE APPROACHES TO PROBLEM SOLVING 2
- WHAT WOULD YOU DO? 3
- A CHECK LIST TO ENCOURAGE CREATIVE THINKING 4
- WORDS AND PHRASES THAT BREED AND AID IDEA PRODUCTION 5
- SPRINGBOARDS TO DIVERGENT THINKING
  - THINK ABOUT IT 6
  - LIST MAKING 7
  - BRAINSTORMING GUIDE 8
- GAMES THAT SHARPEN LOGICAL THINKING SKILLS 8
- TWENTY-FIVE SYSTEMS FOR ENCODING OR CIPHERING 9
- A GUIDE FOR DECODING SUBSTITUTE CIPHER SYSTEMS 11
- SYMBOLS AND SIGNS 12
- ANALOGIES 13
- WORD GAMES TO CREATE FOR EXERCISE IN LOGICAL THINKING 14

SOME COMMON SENSE APPROACHES TO PROBLEM SOLVING

- Avoid prejudices based on past experiences or limited understanding of the specific problem.

- Defer judgment until you have all the facts.

- Approach the problem in a positive and confident manner.

- Look at the problem from a "futuristic" perspective to determine if the projected solution will make sense in the future.

- Consider all possible solutions before zeroing in on the best three. Begin the "consideration" process anew, and rank the best three in 1-2-3 order.

- Organize all the data related to the problem, and categorize it as to "very important," "important," and "not important" in terms of a possible solution.

- Trust your intuition, and use it as a cornerstone for developing a strategy for problem solving. Remember, however, a cornerstone is only the beginning point. Don't neglect to examine, evaluate, and plan on the basis of all the real data available.

- Be willing to devote the time, energy and personal commitment to creative problem solving.

- Internalize the problem before considering solution possibilities.

- Outline the problem and the proposed solution. Establish realistic goals, and develop a check list and time frame to use as a guide to goal fulfillment.

- Examine the projected solution in terms of your responsibilities and life style to make sure the plan is a realistic one.

- Talk the problem over with someone whose judgment and problem-solving ability you respect. State the problem as openly and objectively as possible, and solicit constructive comments and analysis, not opinionated suggestions.

- Do not entertain plans for a partial solution or a stop-gap measure. This kind of action will only force you to begin the entire problem-solving process anew at a less opportune time.

- Write down the problem and all the possible solutions. This will help you to segregate the real issues, and to evaluate more clearly the implications of each possible solution.

- Develop a back-up strategy for a proposed solution. In the event your first approach begins to falter, move to your back-up immediately and positively.

WHAT WOULD YOU DO?

Write one complete sentence that suggests two ways to handle each of the following situations—one proposing a poor solution, and one proposing a good solution.

1. You were being chased by an elephant.
2. You received a nasty letter from a stranger.
3. You inherited a million dollars.
4. You met a fire-eating dragon face to face.
5. You found yourself in a haunted house at midnight.
6. The principal asked you to take charge of the entire school for a day.
7. Someone handed you three double-dip ice cream cones at noon on a hot day.
8. You found yourself lost in a deep, dark forest.
9. You had to walk to school during a rain shower with no umbrella or raincoat.
10. The only food you had to eat for a week was asparagus.
11. Someone left a tiny puppy in a basket on your doorstep.
12. You were accused of a crime you didn't commit.
13. You found a wallet containing three one-hundred dollar bills on the sidewalk.
14. A fairy godmother suddenly appeared to grant one wish for you.
15. Your best friend was quarantined with a contagious disease for a month.
16. You were asked to spend a week on tour with the president of your country.
17. All the books in the world were destroyed.
18. You broke out in a rash from head to toe on the doctor's day off.
19. You had to cross a river without a bridge or a boat.
20. You met a real live leprechaun at midnight on the eve of St. Patrick's Day.
21. It rained continuously for forty days and forty nights.
22. While fishing in a pond near your home, you hooked an alligator.
23. Someone delivered sixty-nine crates of ripe tomatoes to your house.
24. A neighbor gave you a map of the neighborhood with an X marking the spot where a hidden treasure is supposedly buried.
25. You opened the kitchen door early one morning to find a huge banner proclaiming you "Citizen of the Day."
26. After a sudden rain, you followed a rainbow to its end, and found a real pot of gold with instructions to spend it all before nightfall.
27. The king of a very important country asked you to live in the palace and be his chief assistant for onr year.
28. You found yourself responsible for planning an after-school educational program for all the children under twelve in your town.
29. None of the trees in the world had names, and, without help, you had to write a book naming and describing each tree.
30. You awakened at your school desk and were told that you had been asleep for six weeks.
31. Someone gave you a magic airplane ticket with which you could travel to any place in the world. One catch: it's a one-way ticket only!
32. You are performing on a stage before thousands of people, and your trousers fall down.
33. You are making an emergency trip down a two-lane mountain road, and you find a huge boulder blocking the road.

A CHECK LIST TO ENCOURAGE CREATIVE THINKING

Try something new each week.	
Write down weekly goals, and evaluate goal achievement regularly.	
Write down one thing that bothers you, and write a proposed plan for changing it.	
Read one easy book and one hard book.	
Keep a daily journal.	
Talk to three people about a topic that interests you. Compare and contrast their opinions.	
Read a daily newspaper.	
Read two different newspaper accounts of a news event, and compare the two.	
Read an editorial from the Sunday newspaper. Question the position taken, and mentally take your own stand.	
Poll your classmates on a topic of current interest. Graph or chart the results.	
Add ten new words to your vocabulary.	
Write an original poem, story, or song. Reread it a day later, and try to make it more interesting or exciting.	
Learn something new about a city or country.	
Study the life and times of a famous person.	
Select a subject to research. Use three different sources, and summarize your findings.	
Create a new code, and share it.	
Participate in a good brainstorming session.	
Select one current event from the news, and predict what will happen in the next seven days. Write your prediction down, and check it against the actual happenings at the end of the week.	
Do a page of difficult math problems.	
Keep a sequential record of some aspect of your environment (growth of a plant; the weather, etc.). Review the record, note changes, and the causes and effects of the changes.	
Make out a creative but realistic budget for the week.	
Work a word puzzle.	
Make up a word puzzle, and ask someone to solve it.	
Evaluate your progress in school.	
Make something out of three-dimensional materials.	
Make a list of things to do next week—some practical and some just-for-fun things.	
Share an imaginative, unusual, or "way-out" idea with someone. Note the reaction.	
Make a list of three questions you'd like to find answers for in the coming week.	
Observe the behavior of someone your own age over a period of several hours. Think about the causes and consequences of the behavior.	
Experiment to find new uses for common household products.	

WORDS AND PHRASES THAT BREED AND AID IDEA PRODUCTION

illustrate	diagram	organize	extend	magnify
subtract	alter	substitute	extrude	rearrange
fallen	minimize	integrate	transpose	flatten
adapt	abstract	eliminate	unify	modify
symbolize	add	segregate	reverse	invert
rotate	translate	stretch	separate	distort
complement	elaborate	dissect	combine	squeeze
multiply	freeze	thicken	lighten	relate
increase	decrease	regulate	turn	convert
alter	shift	modulate	mold	stain
modernize	variegated	mutate	revolutionize	arrange
superimpose	recast	affirm	edit	vary
revamp	patch	adjust	impair	mar
bend	strain	twist	adulterate	dye
denature	cover	mask	disguise	shuffle
conceal	transfigure	reorder	crossbreed	process

Name as many things as possible that _____.

How many ways can you think of to _____?

What are all the meanings you can think of for _____?

How many different ways can you express _____?

List every fact you can think of related to _____.

The answer is _____. List as many questions as you can think of for which that is the answer.

What are all the words you could use instead of _____?

How many different ways can you show _____?

How would this look to a _____?

What would happen if _____?

How is _____ like _____?

How would you feel if _____?

How would this be viewed by _____?

How would someone else feel if you _____?

THINK ABOUT IT—SPRINGBOARDS TO DIVERGENT THINKING

Think about it . . . then, give a good answer for each situation.

1. If you bit into a solid gold coin while eating a pancake in a restaurant, who would own the coin—you or the restaurant owner? Why?

2. If your brand-new flashlight exploded, causing a fire which completely destroyed a friend's bicycle parked in your neighbor's front yard, who would be legally responsible for replacing the bicycle—you, your friend, or the manufacturer of the flashlight? Why?

3. If Peter picked a peck of peppers in Paul's pepper patch; and Paul picked ½ bushel of peppers in Peter's pepper patch; and if Paula picked ½ peck of peppers in Paul's pepper patch, 1 peck of peppers in Peter's pepper patch, and 1 peck of peppers in her own pepper patch; and, if the three put all the peppers together and divided them equally, who would end up with the most peppers from someone else's patch other than his/her own—Peter, Paul, or Paula? Why?

4. If you had no pencil, no paper, and no telephone, and you absolutely had to send a message to a friend in another town, what would you do?

THINK OF TEN ORIGINAL, NEVER-BEFORE-THOUGHT-OF . . .

- ways to report on a book read.
- ways to serve potatoes.
- titles for patriotic songs.
- uses for ice cubes.
- ways to say, "I love you."
- recipes using chocolate.
- names for romantic novels.
- uses for last year's calendar.
- ways to help people less fortunate than yourself.
- games to play with three other people.
- four-line rhymes.
- words with definitions.
- holidays.
- subjects to study in school.
- ways to honor senior citizens.
- educational toys.
- colors.
- substitutes for shoes.
- themes for amusement parks.
- Halloween masks.
- uses for peach pits.

WAYS TO ORGANIZE INFORMATION

- Synopsize
- Make a card file.
- Code.
- Categorize.
- Diagram.
- Outline.
- List.
- Map.
- Catalog.
- Schedule.
- Index.
- Keep a journal.
- Make a table.
- Create a layout
- Make a sketch.
- Make a file.
- Serialize.
- Alphabetize.
- Order numerically.
- Classify by theme or subject.
- Order qualitatively.
- Make a time line.
- Order sequentially.
- Make a mock-up.

LIST MAKING—A SPRINGBOARD TO DIVERGENT THINKING

Make a list of:

1. Twenty ways to move a heavy box from one room to another.
2. Fifteen uses for a potato masher (other than mashing potatoes).
3. Forty-nine four-syllable words.
4. Sixteen uses for or things to do with an old newspaper.
5. Foods from countries other than your own (list the country for each).
6. Six places in your own community where you could go to observe animals in their natural habitats.
7. The full names of sixteen people over seventy years old.
8. Ten toys that would be safe for a year-old baby to play with.
9. Five ways to put out a fire.
10. Twenty-nine minerals.
11. Fifty-two vegetables (two that begin with each letter in the alphabet).
12. Fourteen words that name something to be worn on a person's head.
13. Twenty-two well-known bodies of water.
14. Twelve ways to save money.
15. Sixteen things to write with.
16. Twelve holidays (give the date and the symbol for each).
17. Ten sources you could use to locate information on Antarctica.
18. Authors of books you have read during the past three months.
19. Forty color words.
20. Twenty uses for a lemon.
21. Twenty-four analogies.
22. Fifteen kinds of boats.
23. Fifteen things to wear on your feet.
24. Ten things that could be used to hold papers together.
25. Thirty-six musical instruments.
26. Six ways to cook tomatoes.
27. One hundred two parts of an automobile.
28. Nine ways to tell time.
29. Twenty-one careers in the world of the theater.
30. Twenty-six cities west of the Mississippi River.
31. Ten kinds of beans.
32. Eight words that mean "cold."
33. Forty-five varieties of trees.
34. Eight ways to cook without electricity.
35. Roman Numerals from one through one hundred. Then, multiply each number on your list by ten, and write the products in Roman numerals.
36. Six places where you could find the correct spellings of the continents.
37. Fifty-nine kinds of sandwiches.
38. A dozen ways to use eggshells.
39. The ten most recent chief executives of your country.
40. Seventy-seven words that begin with the letter s (without using the dictionary).
41. The full names of all the teachers you have ever had.
42. Seven different kinds of grain used to make bread.
43. The ten largest cities in the world.

BRAINSTORMING GUIDE—
A SPRINGBOARD TO DIVERGENT THINKING

WHY?

The intended result of brainstorming is to generate a large number of ideas which will lead to a larger number of creative solutions to a given problem.

Two secondary benefits are to be derived from this process:
1. Students learn to express their ideas freely, without fear of criticism.
2. Students learn to build upon each other's ideas.

HOW?

There are four requirements for a profitable brainstorming session:

1. All ideas are accepted—defer judgment and criticism.
2. Participants must feel free to say everything they think and to hold nothing back. The "farther out" the ideas are, the better.
3. Participants build on the ideas of others. (Don't wait for a new idea to come; let it grow out of the last idea given by altering that idea in some way.)
4. Strive for quantity! The more ideas, the better.

FOLLOW-UP

After the brainstorming session:

1. Leave all ideas written as they were recorded.
2. Enlist student participation in setting some standards for evaluating and pruning the collected ideas. (The criteria will depend somewhat on the ultimate goal for use of the ideas.)
   Examples: Is the idea practical?
   Can we really accomplish it?
   Is it compatible with everyday living?
   Does it solve a problem without creating a new one?
3. Discuss which ideas fit the criteria.
4. Decide on ways to develop the ideas (like making a model, diagram, design, drawing, writing descriptive material, etc.).

GAMES THAT SHARPEN LOGICAL THINKING SKILLS

BATTLESHIP by Milton Bradley
BOGGLE by Parker Brothers
CLUE by Parker Brothers
EQUATIONS by Wff 'N Proof
MASTER-MIND by Invicta Plastics
PROBE by Parker Brothers

PSYC-OUT by Mag Nif
QUBIC by Parker Brothers
STOCK MARKET by the 3M Company
TAC-TICKLE by Wff 'N Proof
TUF by Avalon Hill
WFF 'N PROOF by Wff 'N Proof

TWENTY-FIVE SYSTEMS FOR ENCODING OR CIPHERING

1. Relate each letter of the message to the letter which follows it in the alphabet.
    HELP = IFMQ
2. Relate each letter of the message to the letter preceding it in the alphabet.
    HELP = GDKO
3. Relate each letter of the message to a letter of the alphabet which is a certain interval away from the original letter (i.e.: five letters following or three letters preceding it in the alphabet).
    HELP = MJQU or EBIM
4. Relate each letter to the letter of the alphabet which is the same distance from the end of the alphabet as this letter is from the beginning (i.e.: A = Z; B = Y; C = X, etc.).
    HELP = SVOK
5. Relate each letter to the numeral that denotes its sequence in the alphabet (i.e.: A = 1; B = 2, etc.).
    HELP = 8, 5, 12, 16
6. Relate each letter to a double letter code consisting of the letter preceding it and the letter following it in the alphabet (i.e.: A = ZB; B = AC, etc.).
    HELP = GI, DF, KM, OQ
7. Relate each letter of the alphabet to a code word. (The code word may or may not begin with that letter.)
    HELP = HORSES EAT LITTLE PEOPLE.
8. Relate each letter of the alphabet to a special pictorial system (i.e.: H =⟋⟋; E =⅔; L =⎣; P =⚘).
    HELP = ⟋⟋ ⅔ ⎣ ⚘
9. Use the times tables to construct a matrix; assign a letter or word to each product of the matrix. Then use the multipliers as your code.
    HELP = 4 × 1, 3 × 4, 4 × 4, 1 × 7.
10. Use a simple grid like this one:

    Assign a letter or word to each section. Note that each section has a different border. Use these borders as your code.

H	O	T
B	E	P
S	A	L

    HELP = ⌋ ☐ ⌈ ⌈
11. Relate each letter to a color. Use colored squares or dots to write your message. (H =▨; E =▦; L =☐; P =◨.)
    HELP = ▨ ▦ ☐ ◨
12. Relate each letter to a part of your body. To send a message, merely point to the proper parts in sequence.
13. Relate each letter to a body movement. Then, dance your message!
14. Relate each letter to a three-dimensional item. (Each item might end with the letter it represents.) Keep these items in a code kit or box. When you are ready to send a message, spell it out with these items.
    HELP = 🥤 🎀 ✏ 🎺
15. Create a flag to correlate with each letter of the alphabet. Then, use the flags to send your message.

16. Use the dot-dash International Morse Code system, and write your message.
    HELP = ...-.. .-.
17. Use the Morse Code with a flashlight or spotlight.
18. Use the Braille System as your base code. Use cardboard, styrofoam, or heavy paper and a large pin for writing your message.
    HELP = ⠓ ⠑ ⠇ ⠏
19. Create a system of sounds—one to represent each letter or one to represent each sound in the language. Send your message in a series of sounds.
20. To send a message that self-destructs, create a taste code! Use flavors and textures of food. (You might use a different flavor lollipop for each vowel, and a different flavor cracker, cookie, or chip for each consonant.) Then, the receiver may eat the message!
21. In the same manner as #20, create a texture or shape code which can be read blindfolded by tactile means.
22. Assign the name of an animal to each letter of the alphabet (i.e.: A = Ant; B = Bat; C = Cat, etc.) Use either the name or a picture of each animal to write your message.
    HELP = HORSE; ELEPHANT; LION; PUMA
23. Arrange the letters of your message in 5- or 6-letter groups. Then, reverse the order of the letters in each group.
    Message: Leave keys in the box.
    Step #1:   leave keysi ntheb ox.
    Step #2:   evael isyek behtn xo.
24. Write your message so that only every fifth letter should be extracted to spell out the encoded message.
    HELP = trutH is ovEr all aPplied.
25. Graph your message. Predetermine a position on the graph for each letter. Then, write your message by tracing the points on the graph.

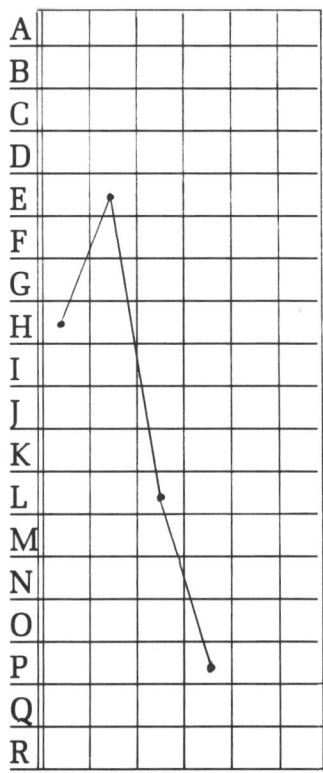

A GUIDE FOR DECODING SUBSTITUTE CIPHER SYSTEMS

GENERAL PRINCIPLES

In order to decode a substitute cipher system, you must first try to discover how frequently any letter occurs in a given sentence.

On the average, the five vowels (a, e, i, o, u) make up 40% of the letters in the words of the English language. The letters l, n, r, s, and t make up another 30%. The least often used letters (comprising only 2%) are j, k, q, x, and z.

The letter e usually appears most frequently. The next common letters are t, a, and o. The word the is the most common three-letter word.

If you can ascertain that the first letter of a two-letter word is a t, the second letter is always o.

TO DECODE

1. Count the number of times a given symbol, number, or substitute letter appears in the coded message.

2. Those letters that appear most often should be e, t, a, and o.

3. If the same combination of three letters or symbols appears several times in the coded message, it is most probable that these letters will represent the word the. By making this assumption, and by writing the letters t, h, and e under all the corresponding letters or symbols, you will begin to see the form of several words in the message.

4. Go back and label similarly any two-letter words beginning with t by adding o.

5. Now, write o's under all the corresponding symbols.

6. Continue by conjecture with the remaining two- and three-letter words, which will eventually lead to the unlocking of most of the vowels. By this time, enough words should be partially apparent to lead to the identity of the rest of the missing letters.

SYMBOLS AND SIGNS

+	plus
−	minus
±	plus or minus
∓	minus or plus
×	multiplied by
÷	divided by
=	equal to
≠ or ≢	not equal to
≈ or ≑	nearly equal to
≡	identical with
≢	not identical with
≎	equivalent
∼	difference
≅	congruent to
>	greater than
≯	not greater than
<	less than
≮	not less than
≧ or ≥	greater than or equal to
≦ or ≤	less than or equal to
| |	absolute value
∪	logical sum or union
∩	logical product or intersection
⊂	is contained in
∈	is a member of; permittivity; mean error
:	is to; ratio
::	as; proportion
≐	approaches
→	approaches limit of
∝	varies as
∥	parallel
⊥	perpendicular
∠	angle
∟	right angle
△	triangle
□	square
▭	rectangle
▱	parallelogram
○	circle
⌒	arc of circle
⊥	equilateral
≙	equiangular
√	radical; root; square root
∛	cube root
∜	fourth root
Σ	sum
! or ∟	factorial product
∞	infinity
∫	integral
ƒ	function
∂ or δ	differential; variation
π	pi
∴	therefore
∵	because
‾	vinculum (above letter)
( )	parentheses
[ ]	brackets
{ }	braces
°	degree
′	minute
″	second
△	increment
ω	angular frequency; solid angle
Ω	ohm
μΩ	microhm
MΩ	megohm
Φ	magnetic flux
Ψ	dielectric flux; electrostatic flux
ρ	resistivity
Λ	equivalent conductivity
ℛ	reluctance
→	direction of flow
⇌	electric current
⌬	benzene ring
→	yields
⇌	reversible reaction
↓	precipitate
↑	gas
‰	salinity
☉ or ☼	sun
● or ⊕	new moon
☽	first quarter
○ or ⊗	full moon
☾	last quarter
☿	Mercury
♀	Venus
⊖ or ⊕	Earth
♂	Mars
♃	Jupiter
♄	Saturn
♅	Uranus
♆	Neptune
♇	Pluto
♈	Aries
♉	Taurus
♊	Gemini
♋	Cancer
♌	Leo
♍	Virgo
♎	Libra
♏	Scorpius
♐	Sagittarius
♑	Capricornus
♒	Aquarius
♓	Pisces
☌	conjunction
☍	opposition
△	trine
□	quadrature
✳	sextile
☊	dragon's head, ascending node
☋	dragon's tail, descending node
●	rain
✳	snow
⊠	snow on ground
←	floating ice crystals
▲	hail
△	sleet
V	frostwork
⊔	hoarfrost
≡	fog
∞	haze; dust haze
T	thunder
<	sheet lightning
☉	solar corona
⊕	solar halo
⚡	thunderstorm
\	direction
○ or ⊙ or ①	annual
⊙⊙ or ②	biennial
♃	perennial
♂ or ♂	male
♀	female
□	male (in charts)
○	female (in charts)
℞	take (from Latin *Recipe*)
ĀĀ or Ā or āā	of each (doctor's prescription)
℔	pound
℥	ounce
ʒ	dram
ϑ	scruple
ƒ℥	fluid ounce
ƒʒ	fluid dram
♏	minim
& or ⅋	and; ampersand
℞	per
#	number
/	virgule; slash; solidus; shilling
©	copyright
%	per cent
℅	care of
℀	account of
@	at
*	asterisk
†	dagger
‡	double dagger
§	section
☞	index
´	acute
`	grave
~	tilde
^	circumflex
¯	macron
˘	breve
¨	dieresis
¸	cedilla
∧	caret

© 1978 by Houghton Mifflin Company. Reprinted by permission from *The American Heritage Dictionary of the English Language.*

ANALOGIES

Five is to ten as eight is to sixteen.
Bake is to cake as broil is to meat.
Octopus is to ocean as tiger is to jungle.
Add is to subtract as multiply is to divide.
Sing is to voice as dance is to legs.
Ink is to pen as paint is to brush.
Brush is to comb as fork is to knife.
Milk is to cereal as bacon is to eggs.
Syrup is to pancakes as jelly is to toast.
Goose is to gander as cow is to bull.
Channel is to TV as station is to radio.
Down is to up as low is to high.
Elbow is to arm as knee is to leg.
Ankle is to foot as wrist is to hand.
Top is to bottom as back is to front.
Yellow is to a lemon as green is to celery.
Hour is to day as week is to month.
Cup is to drink as plate is to eat.
Mare is to pony as cow is to calf.
Listen is to hear as look is to see.
Bee is to hive as bird is to nest.
Gold is to mine as oil is to well.
Pie is to dessert as lettuce is to salad.
Gasoline is to car as diesel is to train.
Tomato is to fruit as corn is to vegetable.
Bus is to driver as ship is to captain.
Nail is to finger as hair is to head.
Music is to radio as program is to TV.
Automobile is to vehicle as top is to toy.

Big is to little as small is to large.
High is to low as up is to down.
Good is to bad as night is to day.
Chocolate is to vanilla as dark is to light.
Shirt is to pants as socks are to shoes.
Few is to many as some is to all.
Smoke is to fire as rain is to clouds.
On is to off as start is to stop.
Go is to green as stop is to red.
Toe is to foot as finger is to hand.
A picture is to a person as a map is to a city.
Teacher is to student as coach is to player.
Centimeter is to meter as inch is to yard.
A ship is to the sea as a plane is to the air.
Ring is to finger as watch is to arm.
Ounce is to pound as gram is to kilogram.
Second is to minute as minute is to hour.
Quart is to ounce as liter is to milliliter.
Writer is to a book as illustrator is to a picture.
Brothers is to boys as sisters is to girls.
Cut is to scissors as slice is to knife.
Water is to a plant as food is to people.
Napkin is to lap as tablecloth is to table.
Capital is to city as capitol is to building.
Candy is to sweet as lemon is to sour.
Stove is to cook as car is to ride.
Dresses are to ladies as booties are to babies.

A bed is to a bedroom as a bathtub is to a bathroom.
A den is to a fox as a nest is to a bird.
A chick is to a hen as a kitten is to a cat.
A princess is to a prince as a queen is to a king.
A lady is to a gentleman as a woman is to a man.
Eye is to see as ear is to hear.
A teacher is to a classroom as a principal is to a school.
Commercial is to TV as ad is to newspaper.
Horizontal is to the ground as vertical is to a tree.
Enter is to exit as come is to go.
Boat is to lake as ship is to ocean.
A day is to a week as a month is to a year.
A cavity is to a dentist as a mystery is to a detective.
An insect is to little as a hippopotamus is to big.
Stone is to hard as sand is to soft.
Meow is to a cat as hiss is to a snake.
A cage is to a parakeet as an aquarium is to a fish.
A bat is to a ball as a screwdriver is to a screw.
Clothes are to people as fur is to animals.
Lead is to a pencil as tobacco is to a pipe.
Hamburger is to french fries as steak is to potato.
A page is to a book as a piece is to a puzzle.
Laugh is to cry as smile is to frown.
A clock is to time as a thermometer is to temperature.
Sun is to solar energy as water power is to electricity.
Glasses are to eyes as a pacemaker is to a heart.
Air conditioning is to summer as heating is to winter.
A whale is to a minnow as an elephant is to a mouse.
Job is to work as party is to play.
Crayons are to drawing as paintbrushes are to painting.
Salt water is to ocean as fresh water is to lake.

WORD GAMES TO CREATE
FOR
EXERCISE IN LOGICAL THINKING

1. Use the successive letters of the alphabet as a determinate for creating a list of words having to do with any given subject. Two or more players may take turns, and the first player not able to come up with an answer loses.
    Theme: Vegetables
    Examples: A—artichoke
    B—bean
    C—corn
    etc.

2. Create an alphabetical list of words, all containing a specified letter in a specified position.
    Examples: <u>a</u> n a <u>t</u> o m y
    <u>b</u> r o <u>th</u> e r
    <u>c</u> a p<u>t</u>a i n

3. Try a contest with yourself or among several contestants to see how many words containing a specified letter sequence can be listed.

Examples: RTH	NTR	ACH
birth	entry	reach
earth	sentry	each
north	untrue	machine

4. Create word mazes on a given theme. Use twenty squares. Find words by beginning in any square and moving from letter to letter in any direction; horizontally, vertically, or diagonally, until a word is completed. No letter may be used twice in succession.
    Example: Theme: ANIMALS

L	A	W	O	H
I	R	C	G	D
S	O	N	A	I
H	E	E	P	T

    Answers: dog, hog, cat,
    pig, sheep,
    horse, cow, lion

5. Create a game in which the object of the game is to discover the "rule" or criteria of the game. The player(s) may ask questions that can be answered with yes or no, but the literal meaning of the questions is of no significance.
    Example: "Rule" of the game: Only questions whose last word begins with the letter l are acceptable.
        Thus: Does it have to be living? (Answer: yes)
            Are you lying? (Answer: yes)
            Was your last response true? (Answer: no)

By continuing to ask questions, player(s) deduce the criteria by which their questions are judged and discover the "rule" of the game.

6. A word category game, such as the one that follows, forces recall, application, and synthesis.

   Form a matrix which presents any five categories across the top and any five letters down the side. The object of the game is to supply one word which satisfies both factors. The game may be played against an opponent or against time. Change categories and letters for each game.

   Example:

	Animals	Games	Vegetables	Cities	Historical Figures
S	snake	Sorry	spinach	Savannah	Stalin
P	possum	Parchesi	peas	Paducah	Patton
A					
F					
T					

7. Create a word game which fits the following format.

   Use a grid of twenty-five squares. Provide twenty-five letters. The letters must be entered in the squares so as to form 2-, 3-, 4-, and 5-letter words which will read correctly both vertically and horizontally. Each letter must be used, and may be used only once. Each word is worth five points. Two points are subtracted for each letter not used. The player who has the most points wins.
   Example: E E N O T S P A P E O T L A E N R O S T A E E N E

S	T	R	A	P
O				
A				
S				
T				

8. Fluency in association is greatly stimulated by this game. Make two lists of words. Write them opposite each other with three or four blanks between them. Fill in the blanks so that each word across will have some meaningful relationship with the word preceding it and the word following it.

   Examples:

sour	lemon	twist	dance	shoe
cloud	rain	hat	Easter	rabbit
desk				view
cat				cry
race				trip

15